You must be connected to earth to read tł wire. Reader, get yourself grounded and then open these pages. The Body: Oracle of Memory reveals that all limitations of the body, mind, spirit, even the barriers of time are false. I trust the body and its wisdom, and mine, as I read these poems, pebbled over in goose bumps, chills coursing over my skin as if a thousand arrows leading to verification of the veracity of each line. This collection offers us lyric memoir and poem as spell casting into the highest possibility of ourselves. Mikell deftly composes a symphony on the page, using a keen ear for music and eye for scoring the reader's breath, so as to invite you into a shared recitation of her magic. She demonstrates her expert technical skill in meter, line, and stanza, while also infusing the page with performative power. You will be changed by reading, by being within the world of these words of manifestation and realization. It is the new foundation.
—Dr. Raina J. León, author of *Black God Mother This Body*, Professor & Cave Canum Fellow

These verses by Tureeda Mikell sing the centuries of abuse and exploitation of Black bodies with utmost storytelling prowess, lustrous clarity, and galactic tone. She is Cosmic Mother, *Iyami Aje*. Poems of pain, as presented by Mikell, sting as they heal; even the funny ones slap. The subcutaneous wounds of memory can hide no longer—Mikell ruthlessly opens them with pure warrior priestess fire for complete healing. Behold her medicine of word: Nothing less than transcendence.
—Youssef Alaoui, filmmaker and author of *Fiercer Monsters*

Lyrical, poetic wordplay. Like the goddess Ishtar, Tureeda Mikell spins many stories through her spellbound choice of words that would make the ancestors proud. Both powerful and philosophical, *The Body: Oracle of Memory* must be read by all lovers of poetry and the power of the written word.
—Robert Alexander, author of *I Ain't Your Uncle*, playwright and visiting scholar

Tureeda Mikell has done it again. If you enjoyed *Synchronicity: The Oracle of Sun Medicine*, you will love *The Body: Oracle of Memory*. Tureeda, a veritable Story Medicine Woman, embodies routes to healing as she explores painful truths from child abuse to genocide so that the "horrors and ironies" in the poems create "a specific socio-logic impact." Mikell's poems take the reader on a journey through past and present to "sense the warning signs" while she deftly utilizes memory as medicine, memory as weapon, and memory as scalpel cutting our way to the truth. She teaches history and reacquaints us with ancestors while enhancing our "sense-abilities", so we end up experiencing the ineffable and seeing the unseen. Tureeda Mikell's collection delineates paths to healing that open when we listen to our bodies and listen through our bodies. *The Body: Oracle of Memory* shows us where we've come from and points out where we should be headed.

—Yeva Johnson, author of *Analog Poet Blues*, musician and physician

The poems in Tureeda Mikell's second full-length collection, *The Body: Oracle of Memory*, offer the reader powerful and provocative meditations on race, history, nature, healing, and spirituality. This much-anticipated book opens with "Oracle recalls / Histology remembers / Body wisdom's cup" and what follows are poems that are recollections that span East Oakland, childhood, and autobiographical references to a life of engagement with art, education, and activism. Storyteller, healer, and truthteller, Mikell challenges and questions the institutions of church and religion, government and lawmakers. In "LOVE MY ENEMIES," Mikell asks: "Force the enemy to love me? / Play Jesus nailed to the cross / Despite the loss of land, family / Language vision / Knowing justice system / Jails one in 33 providing / New plantations for Wall Street." These are works that swoop and thrum with energy and outrage. In the chant, "Mama Coatl," she intones, "We heard you Mama Coatl / We will not forget / Resistance is explicit my sister!" This bold and urgent collection reaffirms Mikell's commitment to social justice while using the language of poetry as a "heavy dose of light medicine."

—Maw Shein Win, author of *Storage Unit for the Spirit House*, U.S.F. Professor and Poet Laureate Emeritus based in Albany, Ca.

Tureeda Mikell's *The Body: Oracle of Memory* is sacred storytelling, equal parts parable, and dream. Mikell weaves the music and storytelling in her unique style that deftly manipulates contemporary life, nature, scripture, and ancestral language.

The work in *The Body* defies flattening. It pulses with rhythm and complexity. In I HEARD THEM SAY, Mikell words rhyme an exorcism of the contradiction inherent in the everyday racism of America.

> *Kill when I tell you to kill . . . . . !*
> *I'm the subliminal criminal,*
> *You can't catch me . . . . . .*
> *You do time for me in the penitentiary!*

And yet, as I read through the body, it's clear that this work is a call to collective healing, which cannot be done before the truth is told.

The Body is at times a story of what Mikell sees through a child's eyes and at other times an indictment on our world, at times artfully both. Despite painful scenes, readers will find what I found, a lyrical ode to the beauty that Mikell sees all around us, and herself, a beckoning to see our world with wonder, love, and hope.

> *Who am I*
> *to be subject to the*
> *Awe of this?*

> *Who am I? (from Dedicated to my East Oakland Hood)*
—MK Chavez, author of *Dear Animal*, and recipient of PEN Oakland
   Josephine Miles Award for Literary Excellence

To read *The Body: Oracle of Memory* by Tureeda Mikell, is to enter the space between molecules and energy fields. It is to watch the kaleidoscope of images multiply before one's eyes as Tureeda re-interprets words: "tell-a-scope", "sense ability" and "response ability" all taking on new meanings in her personal, creative vernacular. She collects and connects history and philosophy in her stories and poems, takes us along for the ride as she glides through the world with an open third eye. Her vision sees across oceans and lifetimes with what the Dogon people she speaks of describe as, "eyes [that] have not been corrupted". Tureeda sees "psychic gunshots" and "spiritual lynchings", explains their origins, offers a cure, and ultimately, leaves us with hope through her words.
—Susana Praver-Pérez, author of *Hurricanes, Love Affairs, & Other Disasters*,
   received the PEN Oakland Josephine Miles Award for Literary Excellence in
   2022

www.blacklawrence.com

Executive Editor: Diane Goettel
Book Design: Amy Freels
Cover Design: Zoe Norvell
Cover Art: "Clearing the Channel" by Lorraine Bonner

In June of 2023, Black Lawrence Press welcomed numerous existing and
forthcoming Nomadic Press titles to our catalogue. The book that you hold in
your hands is one of the forthcoming Nomadic Press titles that we acquired.

Published 2024 by Black Lawrence Press.
Printed in the United States.

THE BODY

ORACLE OF MEMORY

TUREEDA MIKELL
STORY MEDICINE WOMAN

For the voices of the first day you in eye verse paid attention
to seasons that reason us.

CONTENTS

FOREWORD

Prepare to embark on a journey through art and poetry that will electrify your senses and open your heart to the magic of words. In *The Body: Oracle of Memory*, the remarkable artist and poet, Tureeda Mikell, invites you to connect with the Earth and ground yourself before delving into a collection that transcends all limitations of body, mind, and spirit. Within these pages, you will find a symphony of verses, each carefully composed to evoke goosebumps and chills, leading you to the truth and power within.

Mikell's storytelling prowess sings through the centuries of abuse and exploitation faced by Black bodies with a galactic tone and lustrous clarity. As you read her poems, you will experience healing alongside the sting of pain, guided by Mikell's pure warrior priestess fire that opens the subcutaneous wounds of memory, leaving no hiding place for buried truths. The medicine of her words offers nothing less than transcendence, embracing you in a transformative journey that touches the highest possibility of your being.

In her unique style, Mikell expertly weaves lyric memoir and poetic spellcasting, empowering you to navigate the complexities of life. Her keen ear for music and her ability to score the reader's breath invite you into a shared recitation of her magic, igniting a profound connection between her art and your soul.

Through this powerful collection, Mikell challenges and questions the institutions that govern us, urging us to confront painful truths from the past while envisioning a better future. Her exploration of memory as medicine, weapon, and scalpel cuts through falsehoods to manifest profound realizations, reacquainting us with our history and ancestors and enhancing our "sense-abilities" to perceive the unseen.

The Body: Oracle of Memory is an ode to the beauty and complexity that surrounds us, beckoning us to view the world with wonder, love, and hope. Mikell's artistry defies categorization, pulsating with rhythm and intricacy that invites you to experience the world through her open third eye. This collection is a potent remedy for the everyday racism that plagues society, inviting collective healing through truth and understanding.

As you delve into *The Body: Oracle of Memory*, you will be captivated by Mikell's ability to weave contemporary life, nature, scripture, and ancestral language into sacred storytelling. Her words resonate like psychic gunshots and exorcise spiritual lynchings, leaving you with a sense of hope and empowerment.

Discover the alchemy of language and storytelling with Tureeda Mikell's artistry as your guide. Through this book, you will traverse the space between molecules and energy fields, experiencing the power of words to transform and heal. Join us on this journey of collective healing, where the new foundation of storytelling awaits your discovery.

Ulysses Jenkins, 2023
Video Performance Artist
U.C. Irvine Professor Emeritus

INTRODUCTION

There are more things in heaven and earth, Horatio, than
are dreamt of in your philosophy.
William Shakespeare, *Hamlet*

The Body: Oracle of Memory salutes the chariot's flesh we ride in this red
river called *life*. Waters remember navel to navel, ship to shore, past lives
interrupting present time, bringing forth accumulated memory. Within is
the discovery of unknowns that step through veils exposing concrete real-
ity. These poems sit between the spirit-mind and the knowledgeable body,
conscious and unconscious, as we confront taboos, trained to ignore how
they behave and what they do.

I am offering here a reluctant dance with the shadow world that shows
itself as a magic act. A poetic, semi-autobiographical tale bridging the
metaphysical to the psycho-physical and the political. Not a book of, *Oh,
she's Californian*, but a Cali Aries/Virgo state that demonstrates how each
of us incorporates five plus senses. We are more than we have been allowed
to believe. *The Body, Oracle of Memory* carries you from the spiritually
irreverent to the viscerally relevant, subtly attacking the mental, physical,
and spiritual states of what's considered society's norm, but in fact, are reli-
gious inculcations that attack your body's interior for being self-aware.

If I name it, perhaps it will unravel, be undone. We'll no longer be val-
ued as broken for generations to come and see our extension with earth
climate care as one. These are poetic prescriptions from the body's oracle
that will not shun the body's mind spirit, seven spinal chakra systems that
see. They will pull you into adventures of other twilight zones breaking
buy-bull's law of, *'Lean not unto your own understanding.'* This work
enhances the intuition every human may use at their discretion, using
Nummo, Word, Qi, energy, Tao (way) of being. Perhaps knowing causal

values we'd not be stuck in conventional one way, one nation, under one god, instead incorporate views close to, *Do unto others as you would have them do unto you.*

In ancient times Buddhists believed: *There were infinite numberless tactful ways using parabolic expressions and reasoning to expound the word...*

HAIKU I

Oracle recalls
Histology remembers
Body wisdom's cup

THE LAMP

I came, many of us came
From the people who knew
What sound look like!

Was told long ago by
Dogon Griot storytellers
Nummo is the weaving of
The first fiber skirt around the earth
Made of fire water
Mother spirit sews copper
Moisture heat the seat of all life
Brought into being
So is this where it began?

Was it then?
When life was so alive
I could smell clouds in the sky
Predict rain at 5 years old or
Maybe at 10
The morning Mama died
Consumed in twilight sleep
I believed she walked toward me
Dressed in her favorite suit
Bent down kiss my forehead though
Somehow I knew she was still
In her hospital room crossing over.

Was it then I knew?

Where did it begin?
In 1977, the year of the Snake
When Van Allen belts formed
Balls of light that burned in colors
I can't describe like
Close encounters of the 3rd kind?
Or
Perhaps it was the time
I tried to find the right church
Where thoughts and visions from
Scripture preachers preached
My third eye clarified
Through patterns of geometry
Or
Was it while a nurse
Caring for patients
Feeling their medications
On my body justifying it through
Molecular isomers
Mirroring molecules.

Was it then I knew?

I know I stand on both sides
Of the Living Tree
Where the seen and unseen
Watch over me.

You tell me what you think.

One afternoon walking from
The kitchen to the living room
Front door pulls me like a magnet

I'm unable to move.
  Why?
I could not have told you
A mysterious will
forced me to stand still.

When a voice whispered,

It's a sin to see this way.

Yet there I stood at the door
Where myth, logic, lore
Tell the story from body's memory
Turning eyes right, engaging the
Sight of a wall lamp near the door.

Ancient scriptures long before
The bible spoke of a lamp
But this lamp was without a bulb.

New to this nest I had no need of it
Yet there I stood gazing at this lamp
Without a bulb!

Is this a test in met-a-physics 101?
Why am I staring at a lamp without a bulb?
Answer stirs beneath my feet
Olokun Kundalini vibrates ascension up my body
Lifts index finger... points to the lamp.

First my eyes... now my hand notices
the lamp without a bulb!

Have I lost my mind?
My light?
What kind of intuiting allows this insight?
I've been trained by western scientific minds
To perceive the obvious signs
But again from within
A buoyant calm lends breath
From another kind of seeing.

Lifts both hands to wave an X over my feet
I knew this meant no
Because my head moved
Right to left to right, confirming it so.

I haven't lost my light?
Then what?
Gazing at a lamp without a bulb,

What do you want from me?!

A spirit answers so hauntingly clear
I look around to see if someone else is near.

IT NEEDS A LIGHT BULB!

Worry, fear, doubt, release
Shoulders drop in clarity
I screw in a bulb
Lamp lights up immediately.

WOW!

Now I'm bewildered
Wonder if I'm a witch
Is this a sin
Will I be judged for this understanding?

No, said a spirit.

Body knows elect-trick-al light unsheathed
Would cause bio magnetic interference in your energy
The bulb trapped electricity's escape
Now you're safe.

The light man creates
The light we breathe
Carry two separate frequencies.
All scripture in the book called holy
Holds little truth . . . but these words
Bear infinite value.

The commandment is the lamp
The law is in light
and lessons of instruction are
The ways of life! Proverbs 6:23

SAID IN TIMES OF OLD

Said in the times of old
 Was this story told
  Of life in trees
   And teaching of them that be

Said in trials of heaven on earth
 Some came in the name of birth
  To captain their ships on earth
   And test the saneness of their worth

Named organs in us that be
 Divine marks of many trees
  Said others would live to see
   This mark made throughout eternity

To prove they weren't wrong
 Sorcerers and healers sang this song
  Mended light from heaven's seeds
   So we could mirror these living trees
   Mended lights from heaven's seeds
    So we could mirror these living trees

Created religions, chants, and songs
 On laws of life and dawning of dawns
  Emerged lights from heaven's seeds
   Cultural arts of families
   Emerged lights from heaven's seeds
    Cultural rites of legacies

Said nirvana word song
Is a root, we all belong
  Coming from the word "nerve"
  Looking like a tree
  Sends the laws of life
  As it receives
  Sends the laws of life
  As it receives

Said there's mysterious strength in nerves
Wisdoms not to be disturbed
  Because the nerve is a dendrite
  Meaning tree-like and
  Known in the science of biology
  The nerve is called dendrite
  Meaning tree-like and known
  In the science of biology

Said this story is not wrong
  Check the roots of your language song
  Unfolds the missed-tree
    Of living trees
    Trees of life in you and me

Unfolds the mystery
  Of living trees
  Trees of life in you and me

Trees of life in you and me
  Trees of life
  In you and me!

BEE EPISODES

I
Walking on Piedmont Avenue
Ambient warmth on sunny side of face
Arc turns right
Engage
Swarm of Bees on trunk of bush tree
Near height of me
Draws child in me obsessed
With tiny feet on wings
Buzz buzz buzzing after something

I wander nosily off sidewalk onto crabgrass
Begin circling natures winged spectacle
Bend forward
See a bee party

No wall flowers here
Everyone shaking their honey makers
Flying in
Grooving with the moves
Swinging wing out again

They didn't seem to mind
My big head
Crashing their party
My eyeballs circling the room
It was cool
We were all cool

I step back
Stand up
Remembering an appointment
Can't waste time
Partying with other species
Who didn't invite me

Back on my path
I see hands swing at cousin's wings
When it hits me
Bees do sting

Left me questioning

What did I just do?

II
Sunny Sunday
On my way to market
I open my front door
To a swarm of Bees greeting me
I close the portal quickly
Wait a few minutes
Open again
They're gone.

Next day at Fremont High
Upstairs in the library
Before I could speak
A co-worker screams,

Oh my god!
There is a big bug on you
Oh my god!
It's a bee!

I look down
A nice-size Bee
Rest on my belly
But I'm chill
Meditative while
Co-worker continues her freak out
In wide-eyed horror,

Oh my god,
Oh my god.
It's a bee, a bee!!

No doubt suffering from a PTSD Bee sting

I pull the bottom of my
Aqua blue tank top
From my skin
Just in case.

Bee remains still
At ease, as I walk downstairs
Out of library doors
Facing the sun I tap my top gently
Signaling cousin's wing to take flight
It zooms buzzing toward sunlight with
Dust of me on its feet.

III

Danger comes
Honey Bees disappearing

Warning

Mobile phones
Operating in or around beehives
Create interference
Micro waves collide
EMF
Electromagnetic frequency
Scar Bees' navigational flight
Workers leave hives

Mass media bias
Overturn facts
War games play with Bee data

But figures don't lie
Like these liar's figure

Their finger on the trigger
Of food supply.

IV

Shamans believe Bees to be
 Wisdom's connection to the Goddess
  Communication with the dead
   Reincarnation
    Helping earth-bound spirits
     Move to their proper place.

HAIKU II

Body oracle
Analog memory
Seen and unseen speak

ISHTAR ARRIVES UNINVITED

Blood mystery's liquor reincarnates spirits uninvited into our dreams. The dead are not dead. They synchronize into our daily lives reason for existence filtering through a veil from the other side that tells their story demanding you remember.

1984, chilly winter morning
Blanket cocoons head budding
Through dreams adrift, weightless
An uninvited spirit enters whispering
  Ishtar, Ishtar, Ishtar, Ishtar, Ishtar, Ishtar.

Clock ticks, birds sing
Wooden bookcase creeks symphonic melody
Wakes me into concrete reality hearing
  Ishtar, Ishtar, Ishtar.

Who is this?
Hands twist into eye sockets
Stardust crusts fall when
Black bold capital letters appear
On white background, *I S H T A R*
A voice then says
You will find her name in your brick red dictionary
Her? This is a woman?
Who assigned her name to my ear?

A cavalry of thesauruses, dictionaries
Journals surround my bed as I prop up elbows
Rest on shoulders, extend left hand
Reel in the brick-red dictionary
Wool blankets drape my head covering back arms

Just enough to keep morning chill out
Body heat stirs as fingers flip pages
Rain's scent seeps through door birthing
olfactory memory of beginnings
Presses stomach into floor mat tingling spine stretches
Scared excited I can't believe what's occurring

Yeah, right, look up her name,
It'll...be in...the...brick red...dictionary...
Whoa...here she is spelled exactly as shown
Says Ishtar was chief goddess of the Babylonian Assyrians
A personality equal to Egypt's Isis
Three thousand years before the Christ crisis
Why share her name with me? How did you know?
Her history would be recognized in my red brick dictionary
Why do I need to acknowledge this personality?
I've never heard of her

Left arm shoves the dictionary away from me
Elbows collapse dropping head on pillow
Sighs whistle through lips closing eyes
Tears travel with inner guide asking
Why would her name come to me?

I've worked as a lab tech in a psychiatric facility
Graduated from an institute of psychic studies
Collaborated with Stanford's parapsychology department
Earned a degree in biological science, nursing, yet
Education did not prepare me for this experience
Western psychology's theology condemns this kind of
Narrative as delusional, psychotic, or demonic

I document Ishtar incident in a journal and let it go.

Three years later after Ishtar's initial visit
I drop in on a friend who leads me to his media room
TV on commercial announces upcoming movie
Ishtar, a comedy to be released next summer
Starring Dustin Hoffman and Warren Beatty.

Never knew Ishtar existed, now a movie's title
Makes use of her name
What's even stranger, I'm angry
Eyes tighten releasing waters stinging sinuses
I'm running in unknown territory
A dinner fork scrapes the lining of my stomach sore
Why am I emotionally tied to her
It's just a movie
So what if it's the second time I've ever heard of Ishtar
So what if it's been three years since her name came out of a dream
Now she's a title for a movie, comedy.
I like comedies so why am I angry?

Maybe it's my concern with the church calling
Babylonians the devil's work
It was said in every church I've ever attended
Always considered evil or devil worshipers
On the other hand, the psychiatric facility
I worked in the past might have labeled this experience
Psychotic or delusional yet Ishtar did exist
The spelling of her name came
Told me where to look, it was found
Now here's a movie titled, *Ishtar*
And for some unknown reason I am furious.

Can't let my friend see the drama going on with me
How could I explain to him what I don't fully understand
I leave abruptly with excuse of a migraine torturing me.

Come back the following week
His TV on again, within minutes an infotainment begins
Commercial advertising a special about the movie, *Ishtar*
Not a word nor dream about her after three years
Now twice from mass media in less than two weeks.

I watch to see if I could get a prevue of who she was
Got nothing, no reference to family or comedic skills nor
Impact she made three thousand years ago instead
Infotainment focuses on the actors, the film's location
With cost of production, 40 million dollars
As soon as I hear this in my ear
a vehement spirit speaks saying
It will be a 40 million-dollar flop.

Who are you?   Why tell me?
I ask myself still sitting with friend
What am I to do with this information?

Why am I so damn angry? Did I know her?
Why am I emotionally tied to her name?
Strange I feel no fear. I'm not scared
Just frustrated, I want answers
I leave my friend abruptly again
He asks why.
I say my stomach hurts
See myself out the door.

I'm thinking maybe body's memory has
Ignited our collective unconscious from a past life
Interfering with present time but why interrupt me?
Who was she that a 40-million-dollar
Movie comedy would use her name?

Further research finds Ishtar was the goddess of spring
New beginnings, the origin of Easter
Which oddly sometimes falls on my birthday
She was a revered Goddess of Heaven
She ruled over love and war fighting for body's sense intelligence
She was an astrobiologist connecting heaven with all life on earth
With husband, Tammuz an astrologer who foretold
Many events so accurately, he threatened King Herod's
Governing decision power
The King grew intimidated by Tammuz
Murdered then dismembered his body into fourteen pieces
Ishtar found them all
Brought Tammuz back to life
King Herod, enraged by Ishtar's power
Killed Tammuz again
This time he scattered the 14 pieces of his body
Throughout the land
Ishtar exhumed all pieces of his body except the 14th piece
She spent the rest of her existence
Searching for husband's last piece.

Where is the humanity in using her name for a comedy
Is this why I'm so pissed off?
Was she a family member, a comrade in solidarity
Utilizing on earth as it is in heaven?

Late summer of '88, after the movie's release
Which I could never bring myself to see
I hear a voice say clearly, *get Sunday's paper*
I didn't get it... went about my business
Completing my tasks ignoring voice's demand.

Pause

Recall the movie *Ghost*, starring Whoopi Goldberg?
I know it came out years after Ishtar but it makes my point
There's a scene in the movie where a ghost needs
Whoopi to do a favor for him but she refuses
So he sang an earworm song 99 bottles of beer on the wall
Declining to one beer he'd start over again,
Driving her nuts, day through night until she gives in

My experience is similar on the way home in
Hot sticky Indian summer breeze a spirit says
Get the Sunday paper Get the Sunday paper Get the Sunday paper
Get the Sunday paper ... but I didn't get the Sunday paper
Monday comes ... *Get the Sunday paper Get the Sunday paper*
Get Sunday paper repeatedly until I give in.

Sweltering heat bleeds sweat slowly dripping down the crease of my spine
Pulling over in canary yellow 80s Volvo without power steering I
Get out of the car run in a liquor store I've never been in before and
Ask the Arab if he has Sunday's paper
His hand waves nonchalantly with eyes tossing his head
In the direction of papers on a rack to my left
I find one.

After purchase, I feel instant relief, pleased, but I don't know why
Running back to the car I throw paper onto the passenger side
Don't want to read whatever the urgency is in the car until I get home
Rolling into the driveway my forehead temples rain water
Car interior handle hot stepping out onto concrete
Sandals absorb heat wave feet taste, slamming door I run upstairs
Slide key in lock open portal escaping heat
Taking seat in the coolness of favored chair cushioned

Paper submitted to me in hand, I inhale deep when spirit says
Read the Parade.

It was The Tribune's skinny on most pertinent news of the week

OK, I get it, I'm listening, you needn't say it again
Turning the first page eyes immediately engage Ishtar's name
Confirms what vehement spirit spoke the year before

The movie Ishtar is a 40-million-dollar flop!

I'm satisfied, at peace, confused yet feel teary-eyed
Questioning who rules this air's intelligence, really
Why are you telling me?
What do I do with this information?
I know you're listening…you heard me scream
You're observing me
I love the Twilight Zone, the Outer Limits sometimes
But DAMN!

Who was Ishtar to be entrenched in senses so expressively?
Always giving signs interrupting my present time
Like she's watching…using people I don't know
To carry her name or find a book titles like *Conjuring*
Staring at me from a shelf in the library
For no reason other than to find her presence there.

Fall of 2019, a week and a day from the time I mentioned
Ishtar's story to a friend I call the water company
After receiving a 48-hour notice to be sure the bill had been paid and
I swear before all holy, the agent answers,

> *Good morning, my name is Ishtar*
> *How can I provide you with excellent service?*

HAIKU III
Seize audacity
Your interior knows rites
Unwrap your tongue child

LANGUAGE & FALSE ASSUMPTIONS I & II

I

America says I'm a Black African
Native American woman
 English is my first language
  Yet apparently not my only language
  According to body's oracle of memory.

Given a past life reading
 By Chinese elder in the late 70s
 She said I had done all there was to do
  In China as a mystic.

Later fingered gestures found in
 Asian Buddhist books, statues
 And African Congolese dance
  Progress in my hands
  Intensifying healing sessions.

Later a client advises me to meet her
 Qi Master from China
 Because the movements
 She witnesses from me
  Are similar to hers.

Meeting with the client's Qi master
 I explain I have no name for
 Movements I've channeled since 1978
  Then perform a gesture
  The Qi Master said her Qi master presented
  Who passed away at 108.

She then said,
You've inherited a gift of Qi healing
      Qi Gong predates acupuncture.

Years later a fellow Japanese musician ask
  Would I be interested in rewriting a 1200-year-old
   Buddhist allegory to read for
    Oakland and San Jose's Obon Festival
    Titled the Hungry Ghost
     A celebration of the ancestors.

I agree
Accompanied by 5 Koto players
Audiences nod their head, as a translator interprets my story

Days later walking into a library
 I focus on a book titled
  Pei & Gaynor Dictionary of Linguistics
   Printed in 1954

I pick it up where I'm lead to search
 For words beginning with the letter, Y.
  Why?

Then come the word, *Yao*
 A language spoken by
  Upper Burmese populations in
   South Western China, kin to
    Central and East African Negro members
     Of the Bantu family of languages in Africa.

I recall Africa was once called Dark Asia.

Months pass visiting a friend
 Of African descent in his apartment
 As he walks across dark wood polished floor
 A veiled door opens
 He emerges
  Clothed in silk garments of
  Green, purple, and gold
  He is a Black nobleman in
   Hawaii hundreds of years ago.

I share the vision with him
He asks
How did you know I lived in Hawaii?

> *But I didn't know, consciously.*

We witness past lives reincarnate ring of return
 That demand a hearing.

We collaborate on a 12-minute video art piece
Documenting the cultural links between Asia and Africa
Titled, The Nomadics.

II

I was given a fermented tea recipe called, Kombucha
From China originating in 221 BC, during the Tsin Dynasty
Good for gut digestion, called *tea of immortality*

After fermenting I ask myself,

> *Is the second batch ready?*

Body listens
Feet walk to kitchen back door
    Arrives at Chinese bamboo calendar.

Body did this with the 1st batch
Hand lifts
    Points index finger
    To the same pictograph
        A gabled roof over a 3-tier cross.

I have hunted for this pictograph
In my Mandarin dictionary
Couldn't find it
Yet body identifies it again
In response to the same question.

Is Kombucha ready?

Kanji Dictionary of
    Chinese Japanese symbols
    Flash in front of my eyes
    I find in a local library
        Flipping through pages
        I unearth exact pictograph
        Meaning,

                Complete, entirely.

Body's oracle of memory answered
    From origin of recipe
    And the Kombucha's fragrance was
        Powerfully delicious.

There are more things in heaven and earth,
Horatio, than are dreamt of in your philosophy.
Shakespeare

BEWARE OF OMISSION

*There are holes in the ground camouflaged by lush green
lawns and leaves that trust eyes will not perceive or
question what is beneath it on this walk. Be aware!*

Two other guests and myself approach cousin's home
Weather warm friendly partly cloudy looks over emerald lawn
Nesting three birch trees long thin stems scripting breeze
We see a rustic cherrywood door open, guarded by a locked screen
I ring the doorbell hear sister-mother's feet jog toward us
Slippers' quick flop on hard wood floors welcomes our arrival.

Winning smiles offer outstretched arms opening black shield we
Enter warmth of green golds black red and yellow decor while she
Points our way to the kitchen soaked in basil, thyme, rosemary
Fragrances dress white table cloth on maple counter we harbor along
Before sitting to eat, listen to young cousin share goals for college
Almond eyed caramel beauty nineteen years old
Dishes plate of veggie stew when sudden veil exposes crude
Apparition's leech-like stuffed pink chitterling thing
About the size of her baby finger undulates around her head
Alabaster pinpoint pupils oblivious to anyone else
Bides time to jump in her crown
Stalks while she talks.

I'm spellbound as words and greetings fade to background
Has pre-med's hours of lab pathology affected me or
Am I witnessing threat of a disease?

How do I translate this into a warning?
She nor her mother believe in Qi intelligence

Their beliefs teach have faith in holes covered
With leaves and grass
Bible says, lean not unto your own understanding.

Why is she not flinching, sensing, or swiping at this parasite
Traveling around her head on mission to capture her crown.

Who sent it?
  Why is it here?
    How do I warn her without sounding paranoid or weird
      Or in fear of her life?

Should I say something like,
Gurl, there's some strange shit floating around your head.
You better schedule some Qi work quick before it does real damage.

Maybe I can talk about eating well but cousin eats well
Food is healthy organic and she loves rice and broccoli.
Should I ask if I can burn sage?
I didn't bring sage
Doubt it'd dissolve this parasite anyway
Time to leave we say our good-byes as I try to advise

> *Take care of yourself.*
> *Let's do a cleansing meditation soon.*

I know prayers are what they do
That's fine too but this apparition is hiding in someone's
Ontologic metaphysic hole covered with leaves and grass
Waiting for her to fall in, unaware!

I bite my lips picking skin off my thumbs as fate makes us wait.

Weeks later visiting another family member
She receives a call about our young cousin.

Oh no, when did it happen?

Moments off the phone she says our young cousin has fallen ill
And they don't know what happened!
My stomach tightens.

No, no, no! What did you say?

Rejecting dread, family member thinks
I'm crying because of cousin's illness
True, yet I'm remembering the thing last seen circling her head

Did it land?

I try telling family member what happened
Try to recount my experience with the apparition
I try unraveling left brain non-causal Christian-based speech
In this courtyard camouflaging holes covered with leaves and grass
A booby-trap waiting for someone to play, walk, run, and fall in.

I rush to see young cousin sprawled on the couch her
Left side leaning she tries to open her eyes lift her head
Leech-like apparition succeeds in sucking her brain
As though she were its teat.

What happened? I ask

I don't know but I feel really tired. She said
Forcing the answer from her mouth as though each word
On her tongue was a weight that required heavy lifting.

Do you remember what you were eating
thinking, doing, or feeling when it initially happened?

No, she answers faintly

I suggest we take her to an elder Qi doctor
Day of appointment the Qi doctor looks into cousin's eyes
Parts her thick lush locks places both hands on either side
of cousins' head and upon end of the examination looks at her
    and says

>   *It's as though some kind of parasite is sucking the life force*
>   *from the top of your head.*

Stunned, why would I witness such a thing?
What did I see?

Why have so many eyes been omitted
  From dangers that come?

INSTINCT

They say today's civilization renunciates instinct
Gut feeling...sixth sense...reflex...intuition
I had to learn

I really wanted cream cheese that day
But had to learn a lesson on sensory suppression
That took place in the late 70s

I walked into a store towards the back
Where the cream cheese was stacked
Open the refrigerator door
Picked up the cream cheese
But my hand put it back
I thought my senses had cracked
Picked up the cream cheese again
And again
My hand put it back!

Miseducated by the
Psycho-religious who defecate
Body backbone snake
Tree of knowledge is sin!

I pick up my cream cheese again
Bought it
Brought it home
Open foil wrapper and find
Green mold all over my cream cheese!

Then hear a voice speak loudly

YOU THOUGHT I WAS STUPID DIDN'T YOU!

"Damn, who are you?"

Was told long ago by an honored ancestor
Mother Zenobia

"Child, you got eyes all over your body
   that sees and hear thangs
      your mind isn't even aware of!"

I'm a witness!

BALDWIN SPOKE LOUD THAT DAY

—Dedicated to James Baldwin

Read at Ted Pontiflet's final Baldwin exhibit,
August 2009 at Joyce Gordon Gallery, Oakland, CA

Baldwin told me one morning,
Get up
Rise daughter
Go tell it on web mountain
I gave it to your elder
She passed it to you
Now share what I've told you

Any Negro who undergoes
The education system
In this country
Runs the risk
Of becoming schizophrenic.

Send it to Amiri
Send it to everyone you know
Are you alive? Got feelings?
Got Family, children, people, history?
Are you watching?   Listening?
Too many suicides, drug addicts
Children dropping out of school
We got to move!

Hopi Natives say
Black people rule water
The human body is 70% water

We move people
We are known as the clean-move people!
But what are we cleaning?
What are we moving?

We tune in and turn on ball games
Colored men in colored uniforms
Manifesting a destiny's might
Touchdowns take rights

Thanking the "lard"
Living fat tappin' ass
Legalizing assaults every 30 seconds
Manufacturing war agreements
Might is right seizing fight
For Advertising big names
Pro-prison jingoist games
Homeland nation sings

"Oh say can you see"?

Hell no
Blinding the people's eyes and
Blaming them for blindness
Is a multi-billion-dollar industry
Sanctioned by attention harvesting!

Are you questioning me daughter?
Go for broke.
Paraphrase something else I wrote

If a child is born
in the era of the 3rd Reich

The child will be educated
For the purposes of the Reich.

Obama, African American island child
Educated in the *"best schools"*
Won the presidential stool
Set up as a tool framed by Hitler's rules
Groomed as Manchurian candidate
At thug masters' gate for indoctrinating

You didn't see it like that
You saw it like this
Don't say it like that
Say it like this.
Be inclusive
Diversify
Speak mid truths split in two
Never let the right hand
Know what the left is doing

Say WHAT?
On the same body?
Damn!
So you know

Any Negro who undergoes
The education system in this country
Runs the risk of becoming schizophrenic.

We got it bad daughter
Tell us there's no separation between church and state
But every president sworn in on the bible today reads

Enmity and hate I will place between
Man, woman, and thy seed! —Genesis 3:15

Can I get a witness?
In the name of the father, his son
They ghost his mama woman
Blamed for knowing the truth sharing fruit
From Tree of Knowledge that identifies
Right from wrong?

> *This one nation under*
> *Dog-mama breeds*
> *Hear see and speak no evil*
> *Be careful with its trust.*

Tell it on the Mountain
Tell it today

Any Negro who undergoes
The education system in this country
Runs the risk of becoming schizophrenic

And when you do
I'll walk you through a courtyard
Where a Black man stands guard
Over Japanese hand-brushed pictographs
Painted by way of our long-lost Asiatic past
His name will be Bill Dallas
You will purchase one that means
Heat energy magnetism
Thank him
You'll be magnetized to walk further
Into the courtyard where you'll see

A gallery called Chi
The Chinese synonym
For the Japanese pictograph
You've just purchased
You'll look through the gallery's glass windows and
There you'll find me mounted in abstract
Red, orange, green, gold, and blues
By this artistic dude, Ted Pontiflet.

I'll then roadmap your eyes to the back wall
Where a video displays scenes of
Amiri Baraka delivering my eulogy
You'll walk into the gallery
The African curator Corinne Innis
Will introduce herself
Moments after an old friend,
Bobby Sharp will walk in
He wrote a hit song
Unchain My Heart
He'll present a letter I wrote to him
Will offer it as part of the exhibit.

Ask to read the letter
Feel what I was going through
The loneliness, despair, not knowing
Where I'd be, or where I'd go.

Ask for a copy of the letter
Corinne will be compelled to make one for you.

Thank them
Leave
Go around the corner to Expressions Art Gallery
Exhibiting art of incarcerated men

Mention Chi Gallery's exhibit of me
To the curator, Alan Laird.
In turn he will show you a video of me
At U. C. Berkeley in 1981
Paraphrase what I stated

Something very brutal
Must be said about this great
Melancholy nation of ours
and if you don't believe me
You can ask the Indians
The intention of this country's government
Has always been Genocidal.

He'll give you a copy of the video
You'll ponder scream cry
Be called crazy ignored even sabotaged
Sharing what I've written in this letter

That
In the attempt to correct
So many generations of bad faith
And cruelty, when it is operating
Not only in the classrooms,
But in society, you will meet
The most fantastic
The most brutal and
The most determined resistance.

Understanding

Any Negro (and I did say anyone else, right?)
Who undergoes the education system in this country

Runs the risk of becoming
Schizophrenic

Now, know too
It has been made increasingly clear
That you like many
Have been drawn to magnify and correct
Injustices such as these
That impedes our survival.

Heat is rising, daughter!
Earth water wind tenants are troubled

Find those of like mind and
Legalize your freedom!

THE SPELLING BEE

We attend the spelling bee
The twelve-year-old white male child
Stood before the proctor
Waiting for his spell assignment
Stern stone faced blonde elder female begins
The four monitors eye one another then nod
Bell rings
Proctor says, *Spell: Negus*
Negus? Child repeats

Yes, Negus

Negus, he wonders
Two thin rails form between his pale blue eyes
As young ears begin to redden
Implicating the word, Negus

He softly repeats it to himself
Barely audible, eyes jaunting right to left
Ashamed of what he's thinking
The proctor asks

Can you say it loudly for us please?

He frowns pushing condemned uncertainty
from his mouth, *NEGUS*
Dropping his head slowly raising it
He stutters

Cccan you use it in a sssentence please?

Negus, an Ethiopian King, a Sovereign
A self-governing person of Ethiopia

Negus? The child asks
Negus, replies the proctor

Child then spells: *N E G U S*
Correct! The proctor says
Child's eyes saucer wide
Signals what I had nearly forgotten
Ethiopian friend, Nega, told me
His name means first light!

…and Blackness was upon the face of the deep and out of it, came the light. Book of Genesis

I HEARD THEM

*This is story medicine. Release the pain, the anger,
and you will release potential disease.
In the words of our beloved Ancestor, Amiri Baraka,
"Too much patience, will make you a patient."*
... = Nigga

We are your conquerors
Do what we say...
Not as we do!
April springs
National dog month...
You're my dog...
Sit when I tell you to sit.
Heel when I tell you to heel.
Speak when I tell you to speak...!
Roll over, run, fetch a gun...!
Kill when I tell you to kill...!
I'm the subliminal criminal
You can't catch me...
You do time for me in the penitentiary!
Turn your family against you...!
You lookin' for your family...?
They're watching me!
I'm their hero, idol, lost...?
Superman Jesus saves the day
What you got to say...?

Blow a hole so deep
In your ancestral memory
You'll wanna' quit...!
Disconnect your mind from your wit...

Boxed in my ring to me you sing…
God bless Ameri kkk…!

Celebrating the Easter Bun?
Huntin' boiled dyed eggs?
Here come Columbus Day
Halloween, trick or treat!
Wean you from the holy
Give you a holiday thanking me
For getting your Red relatives out the way!
Stuffed turkey day good, huh…

Almost good as Christmas trees cut from roots
With a cross nailed to stump stolen past
Is how I celebrate you…!

To hell with winter's solstice SUN rebirth
Oh holy night is my savior's birth
My word, my god my religion
My eye-doll son's sacrifice…!
My Popes and priests pray for ME…
Fucks your daughters your sons
Blesses my guns, my bombs, my wars
Not yours…
Support ME, my royalty

Where are your kings and queens…?
Nowhere to be seen!
500-plus years of what I see.
Did my god save your people from
Swinging in the trees?
Lynched you after church
Went home and made soup from your balls…
You still on your knees giving head to my god?

My might, my rites, right or wrong
The 10 commandments is a get-along and
I use none of them to get along with you…!
Treat neighbor as thyself…?
MBA law of exclusion is my wealth…
In god you trust me…not you…!
You payin' attention…? PTSD…?
Hyped…ADHD…? ADD…
Bipolar…? crazy…? In therapy…?
I'm the therapist…
I control your will to chill…
Train doctors to treat your ills…
Teach pharmacists to make your pills…
Kill your pain…kill YOU…!
No response-ability here…!
Self-medicated…
Diabetic, high blood pressure…?

On dialysis kidneys failin'…?
Adrenals fright or flight out of sight…!
I got you in jail…or on ice
For a price…Do or die…
My property my water dirt and seed
You purchase from me…
Where you eat shit sleep and breathe
The cost of living is controlled by me…
Homeless…
Rent paying…
Mortgage interest 9 times more
Than your principle…
Credit…?
Want to buy more time?
Time running out?

Time is mine...
My values count... Not yours
Want me?... Want to be me?
Feel like me...?
Buy a Rolls Royce Bentley Tesla
Jag Lexus Mercedes Benz
I created them!
You buy them from me,
I socialize your scale, set your bail
My rules, my laws not yours....
You're mine... and
You better act like you like it...
You ain't smiling...!
Trying to fight it...
Are you terrorizing me...?
Anti me...?
You're under my juris dick-some
My penal codes afflict tongues
You hear see and speak for me...
Educated... Bitch Ass, Master Ass...
Piled High Deeper... shut up...
Egypt is not in Africa and
Europe is a continent!
Are you questioning me...?
Take your cultural heritage and PhD that shit.
Make you pay for it too
Pay me tuition for your intuition!
Fuck a first-mind instinct...!
Thought it was your finger pulling the trigger...?
Got you hatin' your self...
Semen in waste...
Annihilation, your fate...
Civil rights...?

Citizens don't need civil rights
You're not a citizen
You're a slave with an attitude...
Confused...?
My cognitive dissidence inflicting you...?
I manufacture your consent to repent...
Manufacture your world to be bent...
Colonize your mind for control...
You're in the illusion of inclusion...damn your soul...
You want my woman...?

Take her, and she'll tame YOU for ME...
Clarence Thomas, Tiger Woods
Henry Louis Gates your ass...
Have your woman
Wantin' to look like my woman too
Cuz she wants you back...
Bleaching her skin for that "fair" complexion...

Hot comb, bone straight,
Flatline her spiral kink for
That healthy silky look
Think she's prettier now...
She's my human hair weave wig wearing
Multibillion-dollar industry
Chemically burning her baby's head for me...!
Cancerous brain tumors and scalp lesions I breed...!

In my frame, in my game
On the 55-yard line gaining yards on your ass
Three football fields long in outer space...
Intergalactic stations
Looking down on your case

Electromagnetic static in your face
Bluetooth in your ear
Tracks you in my sphere...
You can't run from me...!
I'm a blue blood cold as they come and
You're singing the blues huh...

Do as I say, not as I do
Resistance is futile
Unless you want to kill more of you...
I'm the invader raiding your behavior...
The BART police who fired a gun thought a taser
Do you believe me...?
Do I have your sympathy...?
I murder unarmed Brown Black men and women...
And receive less time than you for tax evasion
Dog fighting and I be killing you...
Three-fifths a man...
Chaos the plan...
My Mafia, my banks, my monetary funds!
My AMA, CDC, CIA, DOJ, FBI, FDA,
IMF, IRS, FEMA and W H O
Who? Not you...
Homeland Security secures me...

I stole you...created you
Mass market media how I see you...
Birth of a Nation King Kong...
Everybody Hates Chris...Bay-bay Kids...
Sissy ass bull dyke Empire cookie
Lil Kim Nicki Minaj Scandalous Aunt Ja-mime-ma,
Coroner football lovin' mama bitches
You desert for ME...!

Save my family, my woman, my children…
Driving Miss Daisy Step-n-fetch-it…
P-Diddy, Snoop Dog, 50 Cent…
Gangsta lovin' drunk drugged out…
Wrapped in sheets Q-tip head…
Pants fallin' off yo ass…
Light bright damn near white wigga…
All good I'm blessed and highly favored…
Black Nationalist, H.N.I.C.…
Dr. lawyer, Indian chief…
Shamanic voodoo Yoruba priest
Osiris Isis black Sirius cosmic dust
Organizing what you do
Unifying collective truth…

I'm scared of you!!
Cause if I were you
I know what I'd do to me!!
N I G G A!

ABORT SOME

Abortion
Abort some
Who will decide time to abort life
Before birth breath?
After birth?
Months
    Years
        Later?

From
 Racial identity
  Running with skittles and ice tea
   Playing with a toy gun
    At traffic light for questioning
     Standing in doorway presenting ID
      Selling cigarettes on the streets
       On the couch, in bed, in car awakened from sleep
      At the BART Station trying to keep peace
     In neighborhood on morning run
     Child trafficking
    Starvation
   Wars
    Environmental disease
    Mistaken identity
     Gang gun violence
      Suicide drug overdosing
Some question
Why stay alive?
Why are we born?

Watching officials dress tables
Communions their staple
A variety of saviors meat
Praising econ cuisine
Fangs feast on
Governing recipe.
So good
It sucks bone's morrow
From tomorrows
Addressing trick for treats
Incorporating in-dust-trees
Cost to live
Genocide or culling
Aborts sum.

TALE TELLS OF GENOCIDE

Memory is an insurance policy against loss
Memory is an insurance policy against loss
The cruelest thing you can do to a people is
Take their memory
Take their memory
Take their memory

August 2015 Saturn's day, daybreak, soul awake, eyes scan room
Stops, tunes into book facing me titled
Claiming Earth: Race, Rage, Rape, and Redemption, by Haki Madhubuti

Book stares
  I glare remembering something when 27 bones move behind that book
  Reveal another title,

> We Charge Genocide—The Crime of Government Against the
> Negro People
> A 242-page petition delivered to the United Nations by
> Eleanor Roosevelt, wife of the former president, Franklin D.
> Roosevelt,
> Signed by Paul Robeson, Civil Rights activist in 1950!

> *Memory is an insurance policy*
> *Against loss, against loss, against loss*
> *The cruelest thing you can do to a people is*
> *Take their memory, take their memory, take their memory!*

How did I forget?
I remember purchasing the book at a curio shop on San Pablo in Berkeley.

Home, something says, "Search *We Charge Genocide* on the net"
And find Sandra Bland's mother's Facebook page post

We Charge Genocide

One day later, attending Native American event
Table displays brochures cascading

    WE CHARGE GENOCIDE, WE CHARGE GENOCIDE,
    WE CHARGE GENOCIDE

Three days later, invited to Tongo Eisen-Martin's book signing of

        We Charge Genocide II

        Memory is an insurance policy against loss,
        Memory is an insurance policy against loss
        The cruelest thing you can do to a people is
        Take their memory
        Take their memory
        Take their memory

Paraphrasing James Baldwin in 1981 at Berkeley,

Something very brutal must be said about this great melancholy nation of ours and if you don't believe me, you can ask the Indians. The intentions of this country's government have always been genocidal.

The following year, interviewing Kwame Ture, he said,

Education in this country makes you stupid, but what is worse, it makes you arrogant in your stupidity, The Revolution is coming whether you want it or not, we must be politically prepared for what is coming!

And in 2006, 55 years after the first petition of We Charge Genocide was signed and delivered to the United Nations, the late great Hugo Chavez, President of Venezuela addressed the U.N. said that the hegemonic pretensions of the American empire are placing at risk the very survival of the human species. And went on to express, We continue to warn you about this danger and appeal to the people of the United States and the world to halt this threat which is like a sword hanging over our heads.

And what did the one nation under a god that despises life answer?

"And Think NOT I come to bring peace on earth, but a sword!"

Memory is an insurance policy against loss
Memory is an insurance policy against loss

The cruelest thing you can do to a people is
Take their memory
Take their history

THE LAW

Your laws
Do not apply to
Our laws

We abide by
Star sun moon
Earth water wind laws
Elements that deny no
Color, state, nation, country
Their feet fin feather wing

What our edicts
Have joined together
No one will
Put asunder!

IN THE BE

Breathe
In the be Gen sing
Black BA-LAM BOOOOOOM
Beep bop ear eye drop dream
Trans lucent wings
Reverent evanescent feathers
Favor Raven magic
Tether star shine, clothed in
Glitter dark red yellow green
Purple gold mind.

Dance a spiral round root
Tally ground wire imbue
Re member, light seed deed
Drum heart lung tongue stars
Rhythm sung long time gone
Revolution's evolution
You and I verse, plans planets seat
Rock steady beat, arms legs feet
Wave weave in heat.

Moon mounts magnetic mystery
Bring back the Honey Bees, please
And swing low my sweet chariot
Let us ride home.

Heaven's sunflower
Has thrown us in this throne
of Halleluiah parallel strings

Orchestrating DNA's helix springs
Springing up children, prophets
Circulating circuits-trees
Generating generations of
Yin yang prophesy
Radicals radiating
I she' O' Lua Coole' bahdeo.

The Word, Nummo
Will not be destroyed
In the Be Gen Sing
 G force spiraling
   Cannot gainsay nor resist
     The gravity of matter.

MIRIAM MAKEBA MAMA AFRICA

Your CD rests on my brown Burwood dresser
Recalls your melanated feat before bedtime sleep
Your be-bop beat-box raged on Zellerbach's stage that day
The audience dare not say your feathers are not other-worldly
Two airplane crashes you survived.

Sprawled on blue coral floral bed mat on tan tuff carpet
Back facing dresser's recorded memories of you
Dreamtime slips between firebird promised wing
Transporting east window's bullion treasure
Discharging summer heat
Dusting face tenderly serene when
Silence salutes authority vacuuming all near and distant sounds

No birds chirp no wings flutter
No date palm-leaves tussle against the breeze, instead
A foreign hum invades sounding Sssssssssssdst!
Like steam releasing pressure from a large clay pot

        My nerve cells run high pitch ring
        Heart beats booming
        Lung breath snatch expand contracts rapidly
        Pauses ears to overhear…
        CD lift…suspend…dangle…rattle…then drop
        Palms sweat caressing covers cocooned
        Clock stops
        I can't move or change the way I lay
        I'm afraid of what has taken place
        I can feel and hear but cannot see
        Ghost signal fades crackling
        Like a needle on a vinyl record ending.

Moments pass exhaling gasp when light breeze turns me over
Surrendering Mama Africa's CD next to me
Who delivered her deed of trust?
Who opened that channel?

I remember Mama Africa backstage after Sarafina's play at
San Francisco's Orpheum Theater narrating the massacre of
Black South African children running in mass rebellion
From the new language and syllabus of Dutch Afrikaners
Newly purchased South African lands unbeknownst to the children
Who were gunned down for trespassing!

Mama, wailed a cry as if it could stop
The grave digger's plot against life, saying

"Parents should never have to keep burying their children!"

Exiled from her South African home for thirty-one years
Black South Africans, disinherited from their native land
Presently own only 10% of their ancestral inheritance.

How does the Vicar witch of Christ defender of a faith advise
With buy-bull verse that provides the word to native South Africans saying,

> *Remove not the ancient landmark which your forefathers have set.*
> *Proverbs 22:28*

Mama Africa, your other worldly memory rippled waters ashore
Early that morn vibrating a sound that rocked me to my core
Two weeks before
The Ancestral ore rowed you…back…home.

HER SERMON ON THE MOUNT –
GOD IS GOOD

I

God, He, He, He's good
All the time all the time all the time
God, he's good
He watches over us
Take care of us
Watched them take my baby
Rape my baby
Hang my baby
Shoot my baby
Lynch, butcher, burn my baby
Drown my baby
Castrate my baby
Lobotomized my baby
Jail my baby
Traffic my baby
Imprison my baby
Take land culture history and home
Away from us and our babies
Because GOD Izzzz good
He works in mysterious ways
Oh Yes, he does
His ways ARE mysterious
God, HE, HE, HE'S
Good! Good! Good! So Good!
All the time! All the time! All the time!
God, HE's Good All the damn time
Watching them commit genocide

On our babies, kidnapping our babies
Drugging our babies
Make them pray
Then prey on our babies
Prostitute our babies
Starve and bomb our babies
Sending our babies to war
Miseducating our babies
Turning them into killers
Our babies shooting our babies
Offering them up as sacrifices for our sins
Sending them to a better place cuz
We're born broken
Don't you know?

God he, he, he's good!!!
God HE, HE, HE'S
Good! Good! Good!
All the time
ALL THE TIME! ALL THE TIME!

My country tis of thee
Sweet land of…of…of
One nation…with with with liberty
And just…just…
He, he he's good so good
God is…

II
Shhhh
Quiet Child!
That god switched habitats for humanity off long ago!
He demands insanity run his warship

Cut stars from sky
Gave Ankh a hysterectomy
Now a cross we bear
Death commands we rely on his word
A will be done
Kills her son
Cuz this God is not into woman, earth or
Children from womb waters
Nor is he into sun moon reasons to
Season seeds cooked just right!
Her mathematics, unholy
Her knowledge is sin in this garden
Only HE
Can be righteous!
Are you listening child?
Your prayer ends with, Amen
A group of men casting
Monotheistic charms absolving
One another from fault without end!
It is coming to a close
But know this Child

Dog is man's best friend
Not woman
Can you see?
The anadrome for dog
Is God whether coming or going
This spell tells you to
Sit, heel, fetch, stay down bitch
Wonder not why you are treated
Worse than or why you cannot think beyond
His dependency

III

Ask
What is blasphemy?
Sacrilege
Heresy
What does that look like?
How does it behave?
What is its purpose?
Who pronounced its judgment?
What epistemic rims support
The gate of this castle?
What kind of membrane allows
Certain things in and
Certain things out
For its good?
Who will it serve?
God?

Is He good?
 Is He good?
  Is He good
     Alllllllllllll the tiiiime?!!!

MAKE THEM REMEMBER

In Memory of Mama Coatl

Make them
Make Them
Make them re member
Our future depends on us
Our children trust in us
Make them
Make them
Make them re member

Mama Coatl
Your story medicine
Shared earth magic
Held birth sacred
Your daily bread
Made those
Without hearts remember!
We make them remember

We traumatize men
Who
Want us to forget
Human trafficking
Slavery
Genocide poverty
Roof-less-nest over family heads

We sing, chant
Make sure they will not forget
That we will not forget.

Make them
Make them remember
Make them
Make them re member

The food on their plate
The food choices they make
You reminded them Mama Coatl
Where it came from
The sorrows of indigenous
The men women children
Whose forced labor in the fields
Provided empire for banking industry.

We will make them
Make them re member
Our future depends on us
Our children trust in us
Make them, make them
Make them re member
Their one way one lord one patriarch
Breaks blood lines hearts
Rips fruit from wombs
Legacies doomed from language arts
Consumed by freedom to enter-our-prize
You reminded them
Made the heartless remember
They can't make America great again
When this land was never theirs to begin with!
We won't be victim to a manifested destiny
NO, We are stewards of this land.
Mama Coatl, declared.

Make them
Make them
Make them re member
Our future depends on us
Our children trust in us
Those faces beneath the ground
Depend on us
We heard you Mama Coatl
We will not forget
Resistance is explicit my sister!
They will try to outlaw our rights
Deny land seed, guard-in deed food
They will try to forget
But we will
Make them
Make Them re member
Make them
Make Them
Make them re member
Our future depends on us
Our children trust in us.

Make them
Make them re member
We will
Yes we will
Make them remember

IS THE BODY JUST A SACK OF BLOOD

1963, four years since Mama died
Her last words to me

Life for you may not be peaches and cream

She prepares my future
At 12 years old, two younger sisters and I
Arrive at our second foster home in S.F.
Gray Victorian in an alley on Fillmore
Why?
They said I lied about a man who
Sexually abused me when
Sex was news to me
Foster mother believes him
Criminal justice system
Incriminates me but
They don't know cuz lie detector
Can't prove anything
I'm bigger than he is
I weighed 205 lbs.
25 lbs. more than him and
Could fight at 11 years old
So he could never pop my cherry.

Foster mothers' sons and grandson try to rape me
Her son was old enough to be my father
Foster mom tells me
Call him Uncle D.

I'm beaten daily
Wetting my bed regularly learning
Body's sense is pissed off.

Before Mama died of Lupus
She tried to warn me
Yet couldn't protect me from
The disembodied death threats
I'd hear whispered in my ear.

You will die, you will die
You will die when you're 14 years old

Scared, why wait? Why chance fate?
Mother Father gone
Courts separate younger sisters from me
We're miles apart.
Can't see or protect them anymore
14 years old alone abused
I have no one to talk to about these blues
Until one afternoon
   On the 3rd floor of the back porch
     Standing in front of the sink
        About to wash dishes for the
           Umpteenth time behind
              Fifteen foster brothers and sisters

My head turns right
Engages the site of an ammonia bottle
Dressed in skull and crossbones
Another death threat awaits
On the clean-up shelf

It calls…I pick up
Unscrew cap
Draw bottle to my mouth when
  Ammonia's scent sends
    Transcendence transporting visions of
      Those far worse off than me!!
People starving
No roofs over their heads
No food in their mouths
Bone thin cold exposed until
A voice from a deep silence
Swallows me whole saying

> *Hold on! Hold on!*
> *You have food in your mouth*
> *And a roof over your head.*
> *Hold on! A change is coming!*

I feel liiiight
More at ease
Brand new strength is born in me
I break death's sentence
I am set free.

I find my social worker
Speak up for myself
Won't take shit from the foster mother
 Or anybody else though
  Beatings bed wetting and sexual abuse continue
   I get through it and find a way to get away
    From the hellish foster mother state pays.

Years later
Grown, on my own
21-year-old single parent
Attending college
Living in the twilight zone

I see the blood niece of
The foster uncle who abused me.

She asks,
Hi, how are you?
You're looking well.

I'm fine, I answer
But made no mention of miracles
Arriving from that hell.

How is everyone?
I respond trying to be polite

She answers
Everyone is fine except Uncle D
He died of a heart attack in church.

Without notice
I burst into laughter
Books in one arm
Holding my stomach with the other
However with the unexpected joy
I stop...and see...watery-eyed shock
On the niece of the deceased

Timeless seconds flash
As she wears the look that asks
  why I think it's so damn funny her uncle died
    of a heart attack in church?

I search my mind and all I could find was
Divine justice

Then I got scared
There were no warnings for that
Outburst of laughter
Not even a preconceived thought!

But I've learned
My body responds to its own
Sacred survival wisdom
Has rules and laws within a
 5 plus sensory system
  Is a rewind
   Re-run, fast forward
    Bio-magnetic sense re-actor with
     Radio transmitter and receiver
      Based in temple's-allegiance
       Detecting injustice as dissed-ease.
       Have mercy.

So, listen well my children

I died at 14
To be reborn and bear witness

  The body is not just
  A sack of blood!

BODY AFTERMATH

*The body as oracle, catalogue's past-lives dimensions in
rhyme, psychologically hidden in histology's history that will
interrupt present time. This oracle mends present from past
memories into elaborate synchronicities.*

PART I – The Qi Medicine Reading

A daughter calls for her mother to have a Qi healing session
When they arrive, daughter and friend help the mother out of the car
Up the stairs steadying each step their hands embrace bend of elbows
I open the door
Greetings

Daughter's rich cocoa smile couldn't hide the furrow in her brow
Greetings, she grunts

The Mother, about 5 feet tall, chestnut brown
Small boned, holds large dark brown eyes
Not at all out of character for her demeanor
As they walk her up the last stair
Through the front door I extend my hand

Sit her here, I said

Gesturing to the high woven back Huey Newton chair with
Arm support nearest the door they drop her softly into the chair

Mother releases sigh exhaling
Black holes psychic gunshots short-circuiting
Muscle tissue life-light support system's tendons
Arms joints join hands locked in fist position as if

Preparing to fight adversaries that
Evade her vision to see because it's a sin
Under Catholic dictums her Jamaican prayers and
Hard work denies body's interior sense to circulate
Her own understanding, she grew stiff
Lethargic, releasing another held breath

Ahh, she says

How are you? I ask

Good as kin bee expected I s'pose, her Jamaican accent present
Breath laborious, she's unable to look up
As though invisible force demands she looks down
Obey, she is heeled under church construct

Are you comfortable? I ask

I feel good. I feel good right here

Good, relax, breathe

I sum time farget tu breafe, she says wearily

Can you raise your arms parallel with your shoulders?

She tries but can not

How long have you been arthritic?

Bout fifteen year, she answers

Were you in a change-making or authoritative position?

I worked wit ta chilren at ta Catholic school
I see many ting de ought not do in administration
Dat hurt ta chilren ana' I speak against it
I work very har and pay no attention how tire me body get
I notice some don't want me talkin or saying nofin
But I go right ahead and speak me mind

She's a lone warrior hit with past life ammunition
Ropes and chains that constrict her arms' range of movement
Wrapped just below her shoulders across her chest and thoracic back
Area guarding lungs heart vital organs that restrict her breath
From expanding and contracting freely
Qi is breaking ropes and chains that dissolve, reappear
Though weakening it will take more than one visit

Are you feeling any relief?

Yes, I do, she says

I wonder how many lifetimes has she experienced this oppression
Breathing eases as ropes and chains dissolve and sluff away
Layers thinning seem to release themselves from religious warfare
Hands ease out of the fist position
As my eyes traverse to a gold cross around her neck
Ropes and chains break away from all kinds of back stories
The more I'd break and release, the more reappears

How do you feel now?

I feel better, much better, she smiles

Breathing easier, she can now raise and extend
Both arms parallel to her shoulders

I'd luv to come back if I kin, she says

I see the daughter's eyes need rest
She looks at her mother then me and says

I don't know if I'll have time with my schedule

I can come to her, I said

Daughter says she will call.

PART II – Qi Aftermath

Following day that evening
Friend arrives to take me to the U. C. Berkeley
Pacifica Archives exhibit of East coast artist, Fred Wilson
She heard about the exhibit and thought I'd benefit viewing his work

Wilson's vast exhibit combined his work and
Artifacts procured from U. C. Berkeley's basement
Dated well over a hundred years of
Skeletal remains of Native American
Men, women, and children
Picture postings of enslaved runaways
Civil war uniforms, dolls, and objects
Too numerous to describe.

I have never seen an artist depict the horrors and ironies
Of slavery with such skill blending the use of art
Architecture, anthropology, archeology
Size, color, and height, spatially juxtaposing them
To express a specific socio-logic rhythm.

We walk up the ramp to the second floor
Where Wilson's exhibit comprises another enormous undertaking
My head turns to a life-like golden brass bodice
Of a young African woman who bears a striking resemblance
To a Ghanaian woman I know
Head slightly tilts up watches somberly her capture
In trials she couldn't escape
Who was she?
Upper-arms muscular, bare
Appear to wear a dress cut just below the shoulders
Walking closer I stand back and notice another sculpture of
A life-size nun looking down on the golden African woman
She wears the mother Madonna image calm appearance
Expresses authority opposing the torso of the armless legless African
Nun's garment, an elaborate floor-length veil of indigo blue
Intricately embossed gold floral pattern beneath white habit
Extends the length of her back to the floor
It was as if I could hear the nun say
> *Behave sinner*
> *Pray to my father so that your soul may be saved.*

Dry bitter taste accumulates on tongue's stormy history
Wind whipped transmigration witnessing enmity and hate
Placed between man, woman, seed and family
The nun says
> *Shhh, judge not! Judgment is at hand*
> *Fall to your knees, sinner.*

Ancestor's blood forbids knees to bend
In presence of missionaries I
look for a place to sit lie down or rest
But there is no resting-place
I lose track of my friend

Lost in the journeys of this exhibit
Past life interrupts present time
Heart pounding chest swells tightens
Waters bleed cold sweat
Tears stream cleansing debris of Golden African woman
I now clearly see she is not wearing a dress cut
Just below her shoulders, hell, it's not even a dress
They're ropes and chains, ropes and chains
In the exact position released from the mother the day before
Ropes and chains my eyes wanted to see
As a beautiful dress wrapped just below her shoulders
Until I see the nun point her holy emissary finger
The finger that directs, scolds, ridicules, and demands their lord
Cuts light circuit souls that know sun, moon, stars' tide reason
Season life on earth as it is in heaven while alive.

I step forward then back slowly tripping over something
Onto cool polished concrete floor hands palms spread fingers
Brace arms as I land on my seat, fold legs to chest, wrap arms around
Legs, rest forehead on knees and quietly scream as I
Watch myself, watch my body recall generation after generation
Conform to guilt from church father's savior they say died for our sins
Accuse earth as devil's home and woman descendants of Eve, evil
Her children born broken, holy ghost her from trinity... yet
Benevolent waters release soft breezes recognizing that
   If our united unconscious can orchestrate
     A west coast exhibit of Fred Wilson
       Who traveled from the east coast to unveil artifacts
         From U. C. Berkeley's basement of an
African woman's brass bodice over 100 years old
   Bear ropes and chains in the exact position
         Released from a client's mother the day before
What am I bearing witness of?

The body's oracle established within its morphic field or
Collective blood memories interfering with present time?

Paraphrasing Naguib Mahfouz,
  Nothing records a sad life so graphically like the human body.

Asking Wilson
    *How were you able to arrange the artifacts with such precisioned
    skill?*
Wilson answered,
    I usually let the objects tell me what to do.

And why did Fred Wilson name this exhibit
The Aftermath
The re-percussion, reverberation, the consequence.

POMO

They steal our sacred artifacts
They label and number our heirlooms
Wrap them in arsenic poison
They say will preserve
Our ancestral legacy
They place them in boxes
Hide them under their
Universe-city floors
Away from our people

We fight for white men
In their World Wars
Prove our loyalty
To our country's heritage
And upon returning
We ask the White man
To give *back sacred artifacts*
Taken from our ancestors.

White men tell us
    We will give back sacred artifacts
    But first, you must tell us
    Their names in English and
    How your people used them.

We name each one in English
We document its use
We supply their request
Yet they will not return our artifacts.

Evil men pay no attention
to their heart's mind
They walk blind
They will have their time
For it has been said among
One of our Great Chiefs.

> *Think not that you or your children*
> *are alone at night in the woods*
> *in the cities, parks or by the ocean*
> *They nor you are never alone*
> *The dead are not dead*
> *They watch us from the other side.*

INDIGENOUS KINDRED OF NATIVE AMERICAN & AFRICAN DESCENT

I heard Ngugi wa Thiong'o compare
Native and African Americans'
similarities.
Native American Chief makes body's
collective blood memory clear.

Native American book reveals
Many similarities found among Africans
Navajo speak of 16 Black gods

8 males and 8 females
Yoruba of West Africa speak of 16 Ori
8 males and 8 females.

Native Americans wear Sagittal crest and
Telephone pole-looking headdresses
Akin to African Dogon and Tuareg
Dance ceremonies

When Native Americans and Africans hunt
They give thanks for the food provided
Will not boast of the kill.

Display of Native American and African
Baskets, blankets, and mask
Are nearly identical.
Educators, students, and scholars many times
Are unable to discern the difference if not labeled.

At a nationwide conference of
Native American Shamans
Chief Shaman displays a medicine wheel.

He asked,

> *"Can anyone tell us where this*
> *Medicine wheel came from?*

Some answered,
> *Shoshone*
> *Another, Lakota?*
> *Yet another, Iroquois?*

Until they were resolved to hear
Chief Shaman answer.

> *This medicine wheel is from the Kikuyu people of Kenya,*
> *East Africa.*
> *They are our kindred!*

HAIKU IV

Sky melds mortal flesh
Earth met the physics story
Trials known and unknown

LIGHT MEDICINE—CIRCA 1983

Light medicine loves life rights
Channels Qi energy intelligence
Allegiance grows shields connecting
Electromagnetic back stories that
Warn and protect.

Client receives dose of Qi medicine
Preparing for trip to Egypt
Day after session she calls
Said she went to bed that evening
With an enormous beam of light coming down
Her crown through her feet rooting her like
A tree planted by waters' secret fluids
Nourishing her sense of protection
Slept sound, woke up
Excited, watchful, and smiled.

Said she picked up bottle of pills prescribed
For malaria and dysentery to take day before journey
She took one but could not take the second as advised
Said her hand would not allow the pill to come close to her mouth
Energy's immune system arrived.

Said she was concerned by body's behavior
Said she had never experienced that kind of intuition before
And when she placed the pill back in the bottle she felt relieved.

She said,
I placed the bottle in my purse

Felt the pills should be reexamined by the pharmacist
To verify what they've prescribed.

When I hand the pharmacist the bottle and ask
Is this the correct dosage?

The pharmacist examining the prescription gasps,
Thank god you didn't take another pill
You may have been blind by now
The dosage for this prescription is incorrect.

Said she walked away from the pharmacy
Spine head lifted astonished, pleased
Connecting body's immunity, defenses see
Protection of light's understanding.

SYNCHYSIS HAIKU
[Pronounced - Sin-kisses]

Splitting left right brain
Synchysis kisses darkness
Bifurcations reign

Sin misses mark light
Non-causal agreements lie
Snow jobs satisfies

SYNCHYSIS TERM I-VII

The Dogons say, English corrupts our eyes.
Anthropologists ask the African Dogons
How can you see Amma/Isis/Sirius stars A and B
know of its moons and revolutions
without the use of a telescope?
How have your people known this for over five thousand years?
Dogon answer: *Our eyes have not been corrupted.*

I

In the mid-90s I purchased a linguistic dictionary published in 1954
Red hardcover black bold letters simply read
Pei and Gaynor's Dictionary of Linguistics with
Bind wearing two circles holding thick dots
Drawn to one another giving the appearance of crossed eyes.

Looking through the dictionary a word's definition
Strikes me as profane

> *Synchysis; a disorderly placing of words*
> *to create or indicate confusion in thought.*

I recognize *'confusion'* as one of the first rules of warfare

> *Make it so the enemy does not know which way to turn.*

With whom are we at war within a society that markets
Freedom and justice for all?

Cross-eyed binding on book clarifies those in control of the language
Need us to see double in other words to *paraphrase Milton in Paradise Lost*

They who blind the people's eyes blame them for their blindness

Yes paradise is lost
Years adrift arrive on shores of remembrance
Synchysis comes to be a visceral experience
Within 48 hours linking synchronicities.

II

At Yoshi's in Jack London Square watching children perform
I share a table with a group of women when a grandmother
Sitting next to me complains.

> *I keep seeing tiny lights circling around the outer rim of my eyes*
> *It's really aggravating.*

> *I know what you're talking about, I said*
> *They say it happens as we grow older*
> *The sclera disconnects causing light floaters*
> *that appear around the eyes.*

As soon as I said it I realized
I hadn't seen them in a long time.

III

Next evening a friend invites me to review a program he joined
Said it heightens one's self-esteem and lifestyle.
It's in Walnut Creek less than an hour away
I agree
He arrives, sincerity in brown eyes embedded in caramel skin
Divorced father of twins

He picks me up around 6ish in a van with other invites
We leave to the valley of the shadows of…

Authentic in his need to help us all succeed
He turns briefly toward me while driving and says,

> *I want you to be totally honest with me*
> *I've only been in this group for a month*
> *I'm still checking it out.*

> *Sure, you know me, I'll definitely be honest with you.*

15 minutes later we enter a huge parking lot
Gray white 2 floor office buildings sprawled in all directions

They all look the same
Is this an omen?

IV

Vermillion radiance reaches across skies nearing nightfall
Friend leads us through double glass doors arms gesturing us toward
Tables laden with spinach, broccoli, artichoke quiche, grilled eggplant
Zucchini, various meats, salmon, an array of desserts, lemon tarts to
Chocolate chip cookies and Brownies and it was delicious cause I was hungry
People talking schmooze, smile, and laugh as blood sugar rises
Sipping water and energy drinks, this will make the mind agreeable.

A tall thin pale man with salt n pepper hair in a gray suit and blue tie
Calls us all in to gather into a large meeting room
Cordoned off by accordion doors that divide the spacious
2000 square foot room, we're divided into two groups

Those in the program and those who are not
Friend who invited me leaves with the members while the rest of us remain.

A stern lean Euro male white shirt red tie and gray creased slacks
Introduces himself and explains how the program came to be and
How it has improved his life tremendously
Then moves a large chart propped against an easel center stage
The first couple of pages on the chart are blank.

V

> Let me demonstrate something. He says
> I want you to quickly read what I'm about to show you
> Then I want you to tell me what you've read.

He lifts two pages of the chart
Exposes the sentence we are to read
Then quickly covers it again.

> He asks
> What did you read?

Some say what they've read aloud
Others say it in unison or under their breath like me
and others raise their hands
I feel disturbing energy
Something isn't right.

He listens to answers then calls on a few hands
to confirm what had just been read.

> He asks,
> Are you all in agreement?

The audience agrees again, voices scatter throughout in unison
He then prefaces his question with,

> *Uh-huh, I see, so you're all in agreement*
> *about what you've read?*

He uncovers and covers the chart quickly
Several times and again we believe what we've read
and repeat it aloud.

> He asks again,
> *Are you sure?*

This time he uncovers the chart
Allows us to read the words more slowly
Only to discover the words we thought we read
Were actually not there

Oohs and ahs fill the room.

> The presenter says,
> *I wanted to demonstrate how words can shift in appearance.*
> *Our eyes can play tricks with our minds*
> *This demonstrates we should never jump to conclusions.*
> Adding, *What we THINK we see we often mistake for something else*
> *Until we view it more carefully.*

True, not given the opportunity to read the words presented
Due to quickly uncovering and covering the page
Appeared to create use of synchysis
Generating "confusion in thought".

Two actors could have demonstrated wrongful judgment
more effectively.

When our supposed indoctrination ends
Members come back to join us as our
Presenter reviews his "jump to conclusion" demo
He asks if there are any questions.

VI

He calls on a member that stands up and says,

> *This is just like the subliminal warfare tactics used in Viet Nam
> and...*

Before he could finish
The presenter's jaw bone clench under glacier skin and
Snaps at man's observation.

> *We won't be discussing that here!*

Then quickly moves to another as many observe in shock
Squints and stares, mouths drop, as though body has questioned
What just happened? Member validated point of synchysis use as
an act of war intentionally used on unsuspecting victims.

The meeting ends due to lack of questions
though there are close to a hundred guests in attendance.
It seems some are still ruminating on the subliminal warfare piece
that was silenced immediately with the presenter not at all looking happy.

A robotoid looking dude provides a pep talk before dismissal.
Audience eyes roll, coughs and yawns ready to go back home
or to a bar to figure out what the hell just happened.

Conference room deflates as attendees blow
Through open double glass doors into the parking lot
While Black man's reflection was denied
He tries to stay behind and fit in by listening.
He doesn't see they don't care what he thinks
A door closes in his face yet
All I could think of was synchysis and its relationship to war.

VII

Silence fills the car as friend drives us home
I didn't know what to say and he didn't ask
I thought about the demo's use of synchysis
Thought about what the Viet Nam vet said still
I didn't want to make friend feel bad about his
$500 investment but he calls the next day.

What did you think?

I didn't hold back

*They used one of the first rules of war
Confusion, or what's better known as synchysis.*

What's synchysis? He asked.

Wow, a lawyer, of all people should know what this word means.

*It's the disorderly placement of words in a sentence
To create confusion in thought, I said.*
It's in Pei and Gaynor's 1954 Dictionary of Linguistics.

His voiced annoyance says, spell it.
S y n c h y s i s, I answer

I'll get back to you, he said

Abruptly hanging up the phone
Minutes later he calls back

> *Check your email*
> *I just sent you another definition of that word*
> *It may interest you to see how it's used*

I check his email that reveals several references
On the meaning of synchysis
All applied to my understanding except one and it
Referred to the eyes that read

> *Synchysis appears as small white floaters that move freely*
> *in the posterior part of the eye giving a snow globe effect*
> *most commonly seen in eyes that have suffered from*
> *a degenerative disease.*

Like degenerating light to see?
I recall the grandmother's complaint two days before about
Seeing tiny circles around the rim of her eyes
Disturbing surprise sweats disbelief water drips from forehead beads
Escaping sun blaze late afternoon the Indian summer I move
To cooler temperatures of living room on the couch where eyes
Synchronize dance stare at a book on the coffee table
Physiology of the Eye, placed there long before
Grandmother's complaint of snow globe effect in her eyes.

I wonder if *synchysis* have anything to do with

You've just received a snow-job.

Meaning, the attempt to persuade someone to do something
Or persuade someone that something is good when in fact it is not
Or concealment of one's real nature in an attempt to
Flatter or persuade or cause confusion.

HAIKU

Beware my kindred
Watch the colonizer's mind
Overhead cloudy

HAUNTING PROPHECY

I
1980, waiting for the 40 bus
At 40th & Telegraph
Elder Black man
Stands a few feet away
Begins his prophecy on
Melanated throne of reckoning.

Tongue peeks through lips taps then raises
Jupiter finger above head
Engages his lingual sword of reference
Eyes close body barometer test wind direction
Pressure measures moisture breeze
Studies growth of green on trunk of tree
Turns sternly toward me and asks,

Do you know the direction moss is supposed to grow?

Illiterate in his speech,
Ashamed I said, *No*

He looks up at gray clouds near tears
Pities me an ignorant child unaware of nature's laws here

Gusty winds whisper
Leaves leave trembling
He leans in as if eavesdropping
Hand cuffing rim of ear decodes
Saying,

There will come a time
When our people will become
So use to being treated like dogs
They will call each other dog and
Regard the dog better than themselves.
Forecast ends

I'm puzzled
What does this old man mean?
Low down dirty dogs?
Or
If you sleep with dogs
   You'll wake-up with fleas?
     Or this place is going to the dogs?

Years walk suspicious of his prophecy
Until I hear

II
That's my dog right der'
Naw man, you da' dog
Whuz-up Dog
These my bitches
Snoop Dog is da shit
Shut up bitch
Bitch betta have my money
I see
Black people in dog commercials
Perform a dance called the dog
Wear dogs on their clothing
Dog chains around necks
Watch them walk more dogs than children

More attention given to dogs than babies
Did you see the TV commercial of
A Black child transforming into a dog
Inside her Christmas gift, a trampoline?

How did the elder prophet see our future cry?
How did he forecast truths self-evident
From the other side?

Fetch sit heel stay speak when spoken
Throat collar snatch
Depends on a master
Eat what master gives
Accept abuse loyal don't refuse
Respond to any kind of affection
Worshiping warship
God-dog-it!

Man walks his best friend daily on a leash
Spreads layers and levels of feces
Seen and unseen as
Effluvium kicks your nose
They might pick-up or
Assign your *soul* to walk through

III
And there came a time
When a Euro female physician
Observing social diseases said

The corporations, the elites
Need us all to be like dogs
It is the only way they'll be able
to complete their agenda.

GIFT NOT FORGOTTEN

Deep reading tonight, Brother Ted
Attended a memorial service after work
At a Catholic Church in East Oaktown
For a friend's mother who passed
A month or so ago.

I cross through sanctuary doors
Face a cross the height of the gothic ceiling
Savior tacked in his place
Guilt floods generations with disgrace
His death ... for our sins
Our waters
Troubled.

Two African American priests
Dressed in white robes
Male and female
Dark brown woman
Light skin man
Stand behind the pull-pit take turns
Telling the congregation,

> *You're born broken.*
> *However, god is the glue*
> *To put you back together.*

Back together?
What does that mean?
Back together from ... ?

I'm a poet, I listen, I pay attention

They go on,

> *We're here for Sista Woman tonight because*
> *She was a faithful servant who died of dementia.*

I'm reminded of something Einstein said
Paraphrasing,

> *Our intuitive mind is a sacred gift*
> *The rational mind, a faithful servant*
> *Society honors the servant and has*
> *Forgotten the gift.*

If you're repeatedly told you're born broken
You might not know you have a gift.
I take note of this while
Sister sitting next to me draws pictures
Minutes pass
Priest requests we sing
Amazing Grace.

> Spirit says,
> *Leave, leave, now*

I stand quietly head down
Right hand index finger up
Following church protocol
I brush past parishioner's knees
Turn left from pew down the aisle toward
Exit doors resistant to my leaving
Emerge under cool starlit sky

Descending last stair
I escape the lyric

That saved a wretch like me

Street stage lights
Spot a young brother 40-something approaching
Beer can in hand, eyes on life support
Like his feet remember iron chains
One step just ahead of the other
Each holding weights
Burdens crafted he cannot see
I wait for him to pass me
Instead he stops
Looks directly into me and says,

>*I know I'm alive by the grace of god*
>*I read the bible but the Quran makes*
>*more sense to me than the bible does.*

He asks a question
I reply
He responds,

>*I know you're telling me the truth*
>*Because my right leg is trembling.*

He asks another question
I answer.

His body falls limp
Staggers backward toward curb
Back reaching a parked car, slides down

Slowly to the ground
Knees up, collapses flat
As if in shock
Gazing into realms known only to him.

I wait
Moments pass
His eyes return to mine
Says,

> *I know you're not lying*
> *I can feel it.*

Time walks sacred
He stands
Asks for my name
Not for money.

Thanks me
Marches away
Strong
Golden
Pride in his stride
Eyes full of light
A gift
Not forgotten.

GIFTS HIDDEN & THIS LITTLE LIGHT OF MINE

Dedicated to Mr. Cleveland – Math Genius

I

Black elder comes into the lab one gloom mist day
To have a pint of his gold fluid siphoned away
This red-brown freckled face descendent of Africans
Tipsy from an alcoholic breakfast shouts

I can beat a computer. Yes, I can!

You see the computer was a calculator to him
Understand?

I lead him to the plasma procedure chair
While other nurses and lab techs grabbed
Pocket calculators for the dare
Elder spews a set of numbers for the truth
Booze fuming

375 x 456 is 171,000
Now, what can you do?
He says with a dizzy grin

A white young man sitting next to him chuckles

Pull-lease bring me a shovel

But those who caught the elder's numbers
Look at him in disbelief and wonder
Until the supervisor asks.

What! Wait! Do that again

And flows the next set of numbers without a plan

$$756 \times 453 = 342,468$$

This time those who had their pocket calculators out
Witnessed his gift without a doubt

We look at this Black elder
 High on his rights as he begins
  To dazzle and amaze us again
   That's when the Asian lab manager walks in.

$$576 \times 972 = 559,872$$

Blond blue-eyed female supervisor
Stares at him astounded in disbelief
The White young man
Who had insulted him
Is now quiet and red as a beet
Silence on the floor lasts for quite a long while
We continue our duties
My lips stretch in long smile

Until a Viet Nam vet breaking the silence asks

Man, I got to get to know you
I need somebody like you
Math in college is giving me the blues
When can I get with you?

I look at this genius elder for his reply
He holds stories he wants to hide

Then recall what my father said
About White men considering them
Spooks they dread.

> *We do things they just can't understand*
> *And can do a job quicker and*
> *better than they can.*

I ask the genius elder

> *What happened to you?*
> *Why are you here?*
> *How can I help you?*

His bright brainy brown eyes grow gray dim
Violation or threat
He remains silent
He had been to the lab many times prior
Though it's clear he held desire to share his genius
Build bond of respect between us
Still he said nothing.

Following week he's clean and appears well
But still no explanation of his private hell

The manager, nurses, and supervisor
Now hold different views
About descendants of Africans in America
Our hidden geniuses deeply rooted
And to think donors risk
Kidney, liver, immune deficiency and fatigue
Hoping for small financial relief.
Who'll pay reparations for gifts hidden?
Who?

II

This Little Light of Mine

Working as a nurse phlebotomist in a plasma gold mine
Where corporate dealers dine
On blood money growing rotund they make aspirin
A pain-killer for bites that bleed from Mr. Jim's teeth
Who visits occasionally to see how his
Human merchandise is doing
Black, Brown Indian Asian, poor Whites
Unemployed employed make enough
To eat pay a bill buy gas and get by
I'm educated for a game to sustain my living
At the cost of another's well-being.

Make me wanna holla hoeing for dollars
Walking floors 5 days a week 7AM to 3PM
Procedure tray in hand donor to donor
Cross check names numbers blood collection bags
Hand to another hand at centrifuge lab
Extract plasma, erect IVs, restore red blood cells
Prep another arm, tie another tourniquet
Open another alcohol wipe swipe prepare
Another vein for vampire reign
Hallowed be thy name thy steel fangs come
Blood money runs deep like the rivers
My savior's blood markets flow
Pay increases in god we trust disease
Born broken I grow until
Little light shines so bright it
Sentenced me for violating human rights

Enacts its plan
Stops my hand
Bio cognitive judge stands
My wealth blocked
My paycheck hocked
It's high noon
What am I supposed to do?
Donor watching asks
      What's wrong?
Cuz he needs his blood money too!

     Leave, said Little Light, leave

I can't do that!
And proceed with invasion of vein procedure
When little Light overrules my demand
And STOPS my hand again!
Overthrows my will whether I like it or not
I place needle back on tray, untie the tourniquet and
Find another nurse to cover for me.

I'm a 30-year-old single parent without parents
Family, or child support
Am I supposed to leave a job
That houses and feeds me and my baby?

Or did this little light of mine protest
The sale of plasma bags for $989 dollars
Giving donors 1% of that or $10?
Was this little light of mine tired
Of degrading the body's design
Switching gold nutrient fluids
For saline salts solution?

Or did this little light of mine
Need me to redefine how I am to shine?

How do I tell the lab manager?
Something here is extremely wrong.

Choose words carefully, tell him

>*I can't withdraw blood but I can*
>*Prep arms and take a cut in pay.*

He answers

>*We hired you for your license.*
>*If you can't do the job, you can't stay.*

Terror enters my mind but not my soul

>When an inner voice said
>*I brought you this far do you think I'd let you starve?*

Light testifies truth
Loss of family, foster care, rape, obesity
Bell's Palsy, little light kept shining through.

I left the lab
Never looked back
Three months later hired as a lab tech
In a psychiatric institution
Forced to leave that job as well
But that's another story
How this little light of mine

Defends its right to shine in Oakland
Where acorns grow mighty Oaks

Blood products increase radiantly
To a 28-billion-dollar industry.

BREAKING BREAD BURDEN

In 1995 at the Center for
African and African American Arts & Culture
I interview 84 year-old
African American WWII vet
Who was a husband and father for over 50 years
Thin, tall, frail, almond brown weary-eyed
Shares his experience coming home after that war.

Says,
We were proud young Colored
Men who fought, died, and risked
Life, and limbs to defend this Country.
We did it in the name of freedom.
This U S of A sent us to the front lines
To protect this country against Nazis.
America said,
Committed crimes against humanity.
Nazis did to the Jews what
The kkk been doing and still does to us
'Cept they use different ways of killing.

We thought
if we could defeat this enemy
If we could prove ourselves
Good American soldiers
Fight for American ideals
Pledge allegiance to this flag
One nation under their god
We'd be seen as equals

There'd be no difference between
Us coloreds and the White Americans.

When we got news the war was over
Blood bowel flesh blown stench
Still stuck in the hairs of our nose
We went from battlefields to barracks
Clean up and wait for buses
To take us to the train station.

Coloreds, Whites, all cheering
Shouting, crying, shell shocked
    Segregated.
We wait
Pay it no mind
Just want to get on that train and
Sit down to a hot meal and
Go home to what's left of our families.

We were alive, we survived!

Train whistle blows
Wheels slow to a stop
Steam bellows beneath the train's belly
Stirring cool air ghost-like trying to warn us of something.

Military guards signal us to board
Coloreds help their blind, injured and lame
Hunger walks us toward the dining car
When out of nowhere a large White U.S. soldier
Blocks our path
Legs spread
Bayonet in hand

He orders us to
  Stand down! Stand down!

Then warns
  If you disobey my order
  You'll be court marshaled.

He tells us
  Find a seat
  The kitchen will bring your food to you

We lose our appetite
Look at one another
Ask ourselves
Why in God's name did this happen?

We were proud colored soldiers
Lost life, family, eyes, and limbs to defend this country
But this country still could not break bread with us?

Hours pass, the train makes another stop
Picks up several troops of captured Nazis

Guess they were hungrier than us because
They marched them past us into the dining car
Like we weren't even there.
Like we were the enemy!!
Like we caused the Holocaust
Like we experimented on Jews without anesthesia
Branded them like cattle
 Killed millions in ovens
  Placed them in front of firing squads and
   Dumped their bodies into mass graves.

Fed them Nazis in the dining car!
In spite of the U.S. government telling us
The Nazis had committed crimes against humanity!
Broke bread with them
But not with us.

Fed them hot food!
Made us wait outside the dining car
For cold sandwiches?

What did we fight for?
We killed for America
Lost life, family, eyes, and limbs to defend America

Do White Americans serve other Whites
 No matter how vile they act?
  What is this White man's story?

Elder brother's water swollen eyes
 Roll tides into mine
  Noting
   The war didn't end
    It moved.

LOVE MY ENEMIES

Love my enemies?
Give them cord to my soul
My divinity?
Affinity?
Life light?
Deny my intuition
Inner guard
Third eye?

Love my enemies?

Let them plug in
  With nihilist dens
    Suck away intuitive defense
Provide
Unconditional love?
Blind my heart
Deafen my mind
Love my enemies?

Deny birthright
Future generation's insight that
Will protect me and mine?

Support high blood pressure
  Cancer heart disease
    Grant America's medical association
    Pharmaceutical control
    Of what is left of my
    Sense-abilities?

Love my enemies?

Force the enemy to love me?
Play Jesus nailed to the cross
Despite the loss of land, family
Language vision
Knowing justice system
Jails one in 33 providing
New plantations for Wall Street

Seriously
Love my enemies?

Open my heart to deceit
As we greet
Turn the other cheek
 Accept dog pee trying to mark me?
 And you know dog is his best friend
 Ain't that a bitch or bastard?

Love my enemies?

The body teaches
I am NOT to love that which tries to kill or injure me
 Immunology is biology

Respect is key
 Watch what you eat spiritually
  Because in the words of departed
  Poet philosopher, Amiri B
  Who told me

        Too much patience
        Will make you a patient!

16 SAVIORS

June 2004, Gemini hands rule air
Nervous system's techniques of communication.

Day ends at 1:30 AM my limbs trembling
Eyes throbbing
I drag n drop in bed
Dawn bright yellow cover overhead
Unclothe world begins
Flight toward dream when
   A spirit bequeaths

16 Saviors!
16 Saviors!
16 goddamn saviors!
Do you know how many ancestors died for you?

      Who are you?
      Why tell me? I ask

Write it down, write it down
Now!
      I'm a mere human
      I'm tired
      I'll do it in the morning
      Soon as I get up
Now!
You will write it now!
Write it now, now!!
16 Saviors?

16 Saviors?
16 goddamn saviors?
Do you know how many ancestors died for you
Before they knew a Jesus?

Ghost run out my mouth
Unknown tongues speak
Left-hand shoots from beneath covers
Right mind sees and seizes picture
Single eye testifies
Countless lives hide   on the run
Hung, lynched, drowned
Butchered, burned, exiled,
Escape, abort, miscarry
Dogs on tracks
Guns firing front and back
Torn from newborn
Renew
We're born again
You have not learned your lesson.

We made a way out of no way
To be
Just to be
 So you could BE!

Your understanding is on trial child!
Do you hear me?
It is on trial

You are on trial!

Do you know how many ancestors
 Died for you before they knew Jesus?

Do You?
    Do You?!

Write it down
Write it down
Write it down now.

You're done!
Do you hear me?
You are done with that dictum!

I did as told
 Until spiritual messenger
   Let me go and behold
     I'm never alone!

G-MA AND THE X MASS TREE

G-Ma said
  I've asked you not to bring
   A Christmas tree into this house!
   I might be trippn'
    But I have my reasons!

You bring a tree into this house
  Cut off from homeland that
   Provided oxygen to a
   Much-needed atmosphere.

You bring a tree into this house
  Packed and strapped into a vehicle
   With other trees cut from
   Roots soil, grounding.

Are you listening? Do you hear me?

You bring a tree into this house
  Auctioned, bought, sold
   Taken to a stranger's home
    Off base, insecure, flat, linear
    Cross-nailed to its stump's
     Severed past.
Damn.

You bring a tree into this house
  Hang Elect-trick-all lights
   On withering limbs,

Place gold tinfoil angel star
   On top of what might have been
   New growth
      Have mercy!

You bring a tree into this house
   Foundation decapitated, capitalized
   You gift with presents, colorfully wrapped
   In presence of family tree's
      Annihilation.

Toast the Yule Tide as its
Pine needle fragrance evaporates
   Dries shrivel become a potential fire hazard
   You throw away a few days after the new year's
   Celebration of the Gregorian two-faced
   Gatekeeper, Janus, of January.

Sound familiar?
How many ways must this
Variable within a constant play?

Let us say you're that tree
   Family, lineage, culture
   Cut off from your roots
   Homeland, language, existence
   Tied to a vehicle with other trees
   Auctioned, bought, sold
      Transported to a foster home
Cross nailed to stump's stolen past
   Your senses sacrificed
   New World order suffice
      You stand off balance!

Your ancestral gifts?
Dissed and dismissed!
 You no longer worship S- u- n light
  Birthing earth seeds food security
  New War-ship trains you're born broken
  War-shipping an
  I-doll SON's destiny!

Dressed in symbols of adoration
 Complacency
  Ornamented in suit, tie,
   Bone straight, flat line de-frizzer
   Blond wig wearing, blue, green eyes
    Contact staring lip nose job
    Embedded in bleached skin
     Wearing a Santa's hat
Your senses crack
  AMA drugs smother symptoms of
   High blood pressure, diabetes
   Migraines, heart attack
   You feel lack
    Slack
     Lit up every night
      Posing for strangers
Workin', sweatin', grinin, shufflin'
 Droppin' every shred of dignity
  You could have had
   Had you remained
   Rooted
    With your native shoots
   Growing deeper roots
    With be-leaves of a bigger
     Stronger tree!
Instead

Your life begins to fade fast
　From a once so alive past
　　Then comes time to throw
　　　Your used dried-up ass out.

Sound familiar?

Too many trees laying in the gutters
　Next to garbage cans
　　Too many dying in the streets
　　　Do you understand?

The light your master holds and
The Light we breathe
　Carry *two separate* frequencies
　Guess which one is not about
　THE LIVING TREE!!

Nerves dendrites kind of look like trees
　Send and receive light electrochemically
　　And you wonder why
　　　Your last nerve is worked
　　　　Every Xmas?!!

It's straight-up voodoo!
　Euro patriarchal who do
　The mythological fat dude
　　Dressed in a red, black white suit,
　　Fronting for Elegba
　　The African trickster
　　　Esu!

I thought you knew!

That's why Santa accepts credit
For gifts you give and given you
Wrapped under a tree
Cut from its roots!
The clause is a condition
To claw your mind, boo.

December 25th is not about
HIS I-doll son's birth
It's about soul-our-energy
Sun rebirth

It's about the shortest day
Meeting the longest night
Steadily increasing daylight!

The Annual retelling of
The Winter Solstice
The birth of our Sun
True Light of the World!

Do you hear me?
Are you listening?

Don't bring no damn
Christmas tree in this house
Cause I don't know which is worse
A fake tree, OR
One cut from its roots!

I am serious
Don't replicate, duplicate or imitate
None of that in this house

Or am I trippin'?

> Nae Nae
> Play that tape I told you to get
> Yeah, the one by that Black psychologist
> Dr. Wilson
> Where he talks about not being confused
> By the variables within the constants
> Bring me that one
> Everyone needs to listen to that one!

HE ASKS

Can you name one African god?
How can you then define yourself
  the true essence of yourself
    the essence of your soul
      and organize the precise nature of your life
        here on earth based on a god handed to you
          by your slave master and say
            you have no slave consciousness?

Why were Haitians called devil worshippers if
they freed themselves from the evils of slavery
  Using Vodun?

The Catholic is run by the Vicar of Christ?
Vicar comes from word Wicca meaning
Witch

Do as I say
Not as I do

        New Testament Colossians 3:22
        Slaves obey your earthly masters.

Which witch are we complicit with?

HE SPEAKS

You mean to tell me
You don't want me to look up at the heavens
For signs of when to plant or harvest
Fish, or hunt to feed my family?

You mean to tell me
I'll receive heaven when I die
If I live right?
Huh?
Whose words you speakin'?

You mean to tell me
You want me to disobey my
  Parents', parents', parents' rule for living
  And Surviving on this land
   In accord with the sun moon and stars?
Are You serious?

You mean to tell me
If I follow phases of the moon
 to sow and reap seed on earth
  I'll be committing a sin and
  burn in hell for eternity?

What's the Farmer's Almanac for?

You mean to tell me
Y'all's lord's prayer
That say,

Thy will be done on earth
As it is in heaven
Give us this day Our daily bread

Is not to be lived?
 Only believed?

 Well damn!

You mean to tell me
It's a sin before your god to pay attention
To stars that mark North south east and west?

When I walk alone in the woods at night
Watching the heavens or
Knowing left from right
I ain't ne'vah been lost!

Ships use the North star to navigate
They talk about it all the time.

You mean to tell me
They're going to hell too?

You mean to tell me
I'm not supposed to lean on
My own understanding?
Disregard those who came before me
That lived well enough to teach me and
   Live to be over 100 years old?
    Huh, is that what you're saying?
Look'a hear
My brother dodged a bullet

Leaning on his own understanding
Cause something told him to move!

He would have been dead if he believed
In what your church school tells you to do.

Blind faith
Stand still
Trust with the whole heart?
In who?
Fo' what?

Ain't too smart if' in you ask me
Something ain't right and
The Earth is sufferin' from all y'all ignorance.

Recitin' verse without sight
Buy-bull got y'all too scared to live.

Everything in and around me is alive
Got custody of me and my body and
I like it like that.

UMUM BUMUM AND SUMUM

They tell us, judge not lest ye be judged
Doll Monkeys demonstrate
What we are to imitate
Hands cover
Ears, eyes, and mouth

> We ask
> What does this mean?
> Do you want us deaf dumb & blind?

Parishioner answers
Hush, "the good book" reads
He sends us out as sheep
  Among wolves!

> But are we to be
> Deaf dumb & blind
> Among them?

"Quiet!"
They say
"Judge not lest ye be judged"

> We ask,
> Judge not who is the wolf
> While we are sheep?

"Silence!" They argue
"Toss not your pearls to swine"

Toss not... our pearls... to swine?
Judge not... Who is the swine?
While deaf, dumb, and blind?

"It is the commandment!
Judge not lest ye be judged
I send you as sheep among wolves!"

But why deaf dumb and blind?

"Be Silent
You ponder too many questions.
Too many questions!
Have Faith!"

Whose faith?

Why are we not to
See the wolf
That may devour us?
Nor judge who is the swine
We are not to give our pearls?

Annoyed smiles answer
Come into our Parish of worship
All will be taught and explained unto you

We question the word "Parish"
Their good book reads
A people without vision
Will perish.

Why did the church
Exchange one vowel to create
Another vow oath pledge promise?

Why do
Perish and parish
Carry the same sound?

Why must we do what
The doll monkeys do?
Why hear see and speak
Without truth?

We question the rules of
The churchman.
We will not be silent!
We will listen
And watch
How wolves *prey!*

SUFFER LITTLE CHILDREN

Suffer little children
Who come unto smells of distilleries
Sugar cane refineries
Disappeared families
For there is the bloodstained butchery
Of cane dissing the abled.

Suffer little children
Who witness child sacrifice
Eyes rolling back to mystery
Blood spilling the warning.

> *Do as you are told*
> *Lest this be done to you.*

Suffer little children
that tremble in terror
Their sorrow for loss
  of a hand nose limb or life!
God, after all
Did have his son sacrificed.

Suffer little children
That look with familiar nods
Yet know the rod with its staff
Will not comfort them
They must use other means for freedom.

Suffer little children
The irony of being alive
While church waits for you to die
To have a better life
For therein lies an abyss
Destroying your existence.

Suffer little children
Who know too much
See enough
Denied loving touch
For they are running out of time
Born broken
In kingdom doomed
By a god.

INNOCENT MEMORIES

*Dedicated to my old school East Oakland
neighborhood*

Warm moist breeze streams
In and out of old-factory after rains
Bearing thoughts of who I am

Recurring dreams
Limitless framed wonders
Innumerable flowers birds trees
Bees tiny winged feet buzzing
With so many you's and me's
You's and me's

Wind spinning earth spells
Pregnant under dark clouds
Silver lines billowing high
Showing off sun water mist
Insist on rainbows

As I, the mystical child, imagines
This is where god lives, smiling
Watching earth smile back
In her black fertile dampness

I'd love to make mud cakes in
Watch my mother and father
Plant gardens in

So many colors
So many trees
So many you's and me's
You's and me's

It's so big and everywhere
I run into my garage
Frightened of who I am and
Wonder

Who am I
To be subject to the
Wonder of this

Who am I?

SCENT SENTENCED

Seafood market Friday
Dark cocoa man-child
Three years old
Walks proudly alongside his tall
Ruggedly handsome
Full lipped nose daddy
On a dinner run
Little one knows
Not to fall too far behind

Fish on display on his way
Catches an array of fresh caught
Belly-up fins to investigate
Many specimens within reach
He tilts his head
Big dark eyes swallow curiously
Doesn't care if anyone is watching
This is his public private laboratory

He begins with first primal sense
Smell

Index finger presses
On armored fish scales
Moves ample sample of aroma
To nostrils that flare
Inhaling deep his
Chest expands revealing
His lungs' capacity is seriously
Investigating with olfactory

Eyes close examining interior
His nose knows then
Slowly opens his mirror on me
Exhaling an ancient being
Far beyond his years

Fragrance pulling him back to
Mother's amniotic sack
Swimming ashore
He transforms
From amphibian to human
Through Vesica's door
 The scent that
  Sentenced
    His existence.

TODDLER'S IRON MEMORY

Try Sunday's bright blue sky
Today not one cloud hovers over
Siena brown family as
They accompany their little one
Learning how to use her new feet
On sidewalk's store front-filled street.

Scrubbed shine-new in
Pink-white ruffled dress
Lace-tier socks in patent-leather shoes
Two Afro-puffs crown her head as
Parents living doll toddles ahead
Exploring her independence.

She walks past the doggies in the window
Past smells of Philly-cheese, fries and
Fresh fried donuts doused in maple frosting
Wafting the air.

Keeps her steady pace until
Her large sparkling eyes engage
The old clothes cleaner
Closed for over twenty years display
Eight antique irons

She stops stares and
Points to one of them
Begins to speak toddlerese
As though explaining its use

Long before plug-in cords or
Her parents' parents came to be.

Engrossed in child's behavior they
Can hardly believe what they're witnessing
Wishing they could translate
What their elder baby is saying.

Her small tootsie roll index finger
Points to the iron as if giving a history lesson
Looks at it then nods up and down at parents.

Guess she's telling them
How hard it was back in those days
To care for clothes
Loading hot coals in the irons belly

Or we think
That's what she's saying.

Baby girl's past life
Revisits a rhyme
Returns to iron
Her wrinkle in time.

HALLOWEEN AT SEEK

October 26, near Halloween
I teach poetry storytelling
Class comprises of 4th and 5th graders
In deep East Oakland on the 90 Aves.

Students enter restless loud
Hit one another and run
Calling each other names
Family members or
Loved ones didn't give them
Until I suggest they share ghost stories
They settle in quick
Quiet
Sharing begins
Fiction becomes nonfiction
And it gets serious.

Dark melanated hues
Sighted for behavioral issues become
Accountable listeners
Faces relax
Eyes broaden in wonder push
Tense lines from brows
 Saying things like
  No, wait, what did you say?
  Say that again
   Each taking turn
     Waiting to tell their story.

No ADD or ADHD here!

Class runs late while supper program waits
Students don't want to leave
They're feeding each other another kind of cuisine
Identifying food from missed trees told not to see.

Ears eyes receive their interior is alive
Recounting parallel worlds of their dead
Breezes signaling smells of big mama's perfume
Cigar smoke stirring aromas in the living room
Secret whispers from loved ones long gone
They feel are still among them.

Anniversary of violence haunting unrest
Time of year, dates and numbers
Of who reappears near their birthday
Or annual date and time they left this world.
Shadows walking across the bedroom
Lights turning off or on
Students know who the signals are from
Class mates agree
When the doors creaks
 The kitchen cabinets open or
 Dishes settle in the drainer or
  Someone appears in the bedroom closet
   They've been missing
    They know the dead are not dead.

School monitor opens class door
Announces time for students to leave
They're late she tells me.

Appetite satisfied they look at me
 Eyes wide plead
  No, we can't leave now.

They'll leave shortly, I said.

And when they do
Peace composes the room into a medicine chest
Releasing tightness, stress
Shoulders drop, voices speak softly
Students move slower as if feet
Are noticing solid ground for the first time.

  The way they came in is not
    The way they're leaving.

No mention of Halloween costumes or candy
Perhaps they intuitively know
Weaned from the holy
Halloween parade is an entertainment show.

Following day, the school principal approaches me
She tells me a parent questioned her son's interest in ghost spirits

        What did you talk about in class, she asks?

I explain how students transform Halloween stories from
Fiction to non-fiction that kept them listening
Well engaged for over an hour without anger or rage.

They were captivated by one another, at peace, relieved
So I allowed them to have a bit of respite.

Principal tells me
        The child's mother is extremely religious
        They don't believe in things like that.

In other words, I say to myself

>*The child needs to sever their gut response ability*
>*To body sense awareness and disengage their inner nature*
>*Because religious dictums say so?*
>*Damned, in more ways than one.*

I didn't combat what she said
I know religion's resistance to innate interior is brutal
Colonial psychology and theology run society.

>*Lean not unto your own understanding, they say.*

No time to fight with the *oppressive* self-righteous
I said nothing but,

>*I understand.*

Following day in class students make no mention
Of ghost stories from the previous day.
Inner nature tabooed
What could I say?

In the Trick for a Treat
Body filled with sin misses which piece?

What does their bible mean when it says,

In order to enter the kingdom
You must first come as a child!

REMEMBERING CHILDHOOD

It's 1994, I'm poet in residence at a middle school
in deep East Oakland where 98.9% of African American
Youth enrolled are in the heaves of the crack epidemic sending
Over 40% of the students into foster care like I was yet
Not for the same reasons.

I invite Kujichagulia to my classrooms to share gifts
As a musician, wordsmith and author.
We arrange a meeting in front of the middle school's gate
Lively blue skies infuse fresh cut grass stirring odors
Masquerading as food from the cafeteria with
View of orange California poppies lining the fence
Pleasing the eyes throwing nostrils into
Head-splitting contradiction.

Kujichagulia melanated hues un-bruised by colonization,
Wears stylized pink head wrap surrounding a cowry shell cap
Topping locks, black skirt, boots, and leather jacket
Drum in hand we walk to the first of three classes.

We're cultural workers, activists
Discussing goals for classrooms knowing
East Oakland youth have witnessed far more
Black-on-Black crime and police violence than we did as children.

Walking quickly through hallways anticipating the late bell
Students run ahead, toward, and between us
Making mad dashes to and from classrooms while
Others carry eyes out of breath out of hope and

Could care less about a bell ringing
Life running late with promise
They wear death mask.

We pass the library
It's closed again
It's closed most of the time
The Euro librarian appears to be a prop
Who guards the tomes as if
Black students are not to get too close.

Knowledge is evil
The buy-bull said so.

Though we know students need to
Hear, read, and listen to one another
Need to articulate ways out of this madness
Critically think and discern the real world
Learn how to cast spells out of this hell
Use comedy, music, dance, poetry, art and
Storytelling skills ancestors willed them.

Arriving to our first class we greet the
Euro teacher looking over
The rim of her glasses watching for latecomers
Detention slips ready for anyone who breaks
The law of the tardy bell.

Forget what students feel
Forget if they're hungry
Forget who was murdered, died
Addicted or what morning delivered
Days, nights, years of known rivers

Filled with dry bones
Pedagogy of the oppressed
Don't see or tell of slow drip's secret hell
Keep it to yourself!

Remember the law of,

Children are to be seen, not heard.

I introduce Kujichagulia, to the seventh and eighth graders
She shares the story of being 10 years old
Her mother, a teacher would demand she go
to the library after school because she knew the librarian well
and was told to stay there until her mother got home from work
However, she was more interested in checking out
A cute little boy who'd pass the library every day
than going there to study.

"It was the only way I got to see
My secret puppy love," she said.
Many students blush red-brown grins
In defense of her story's sentiments.

The librarian introduced me to Black books
By Black writers, lawyers, doctors
and political leaders.
I didn't want to read these books
But she'd tell my mother if I didn't
Facing the consequences of not visiting or
Playing with friends on the weekends
Would have taken my freedom, so
I had to make a choice and it changed my life
I learned about Thurgood Marshall, a civil rights lawyer

Decided to become a lawyer and studied hard and fast
I graduated from high school at 16.

Students' eyes dramatize her drum song call and response
Like runaway trains off track under cultural attack
Their minds run back, dark eyes sparkling.

She finishes just minutes before the bell rings
Student's appreciative smiles, and head nods
Grants approval.

We head to the second class. I ask Kujichagulia

> *Girl, you actually remember what you thought and felt*
> *when you were 10 years old?*
> *I barely remember being 10 let alone thinking*
> *What I wanted to be when I grew up.*

I laugh at myself
Kujichagulia looks at me curiously.

We walk into the second classroom
I introduce Kujichagulia
to another Euro teacher with students
She tells the same story of her walks to the library
Her secret puppy love, and the librarian that forced her to read
Books by and about Black political leaders, lawyers, and doctors
It's just as funny and engaging as it was the first time
Yet my body pulsates an ache just beneath skin
Robbing my attention as if my mind was in an audience
Watching my body on stage perform a plot
I can't believe or am unaware of.

We walk toward the third class
Body twitches and jerks as though
An invisible electrode is jolting facial muscles
Arms, chest, with cramps folding my stomach.

We arrive to the final class
Kujichagulia, the students nor teacher
Appear to notice my physical drama
No one looks, stares, or tries to hide glances as though
Concealing something strange is happening with me.

After introductions
I can hear Kujichagulia repeat her story
But can't really hear her.

I'm in a slow motion movie
My mind is somewhere on a set I can't identify
Chest pains swell like tides rushing in and out
Pushing against skin walls
Feeling taut, tight, about to split
As water seeps up out of my eyes like
A dam about to break and carry me away.

What's wrong with you, what's wrong, T?
No response from inner voice
Kujichagulia continues class while
I tip-toe toward the classroom teacher and whisper
I'll be right back
I excuse myself as
Unfamiliar waters crash against soul's windows
Washing me into another time zone
Swirling inside a hull of a ship
In the middle of an ocean nausea descends.

I step quickly out of the classroom
Into corridors running toward faculty restroom
Fumbling for keys, shaking,
I open the door and see it's empty
Thankful no one is here to judge or see
A tsunami breaches the child facing a mirror
What's wrong?   What is wrong with you?
  I ask again then hear

> *Your dreams of a future were cut short*
> *At the age she recognized her ambition*
> *You thought you were going to die!*

The voice silences the flood gushing
Dissolving, evaporating waters
The child leaves
A proud woman returns
Examining

I severed that past, didn't I?
  I let go of reliving the death of
    My mother at 10, didn't I?
      The rapes, death threats, foster-care abuse
        That followed, did I not?

I'm in control of letting go of my past
  Am I not?
    It's behind me now, right?
    I'm grown now, over it
      RIGHT?
        Right?

A voice murmurs,
Will pain leave you because you decide to leave it?
Your body's tissues record issues for a reason.

Paraphrasing Naguib Mahfouz,
Nothing records a sad life so graphically like the human body.

Body's memory buried alive
 Lies dormant
  Until artist arrives
   Remembering
    Childhood!

THE RITUAL

Spring spirals sprite spirits
Immortal body jumps
Strikes a match
Ignites
 Fire
  Heart
  Heat
   Moisture release
    Chariots flesh funk
    Sweet
     Swings low
      Let us ride
       From other side.

Where met-a-physical tones
 Enthrone homes
 Bathe bone
  Call out
  Oh god
   Oh my god
    On a good day.

Nine moons sanctify
 Array of sons and daughters
  Canonizes flesh stone water
   Scenes seen and unseen.

Heartbeats immortality's womb
 Empirical loom

Spherical room
Lyrical tune.

Joy…pain…sunshine and rain.

Cuz everybody got a
Little light under the sun.

5 cosigns 5 sisters and brothers
Math logic baptizes lives of
Father from the Mother.

Fibonacci's wheel keeps on turnin'
Rollin' rollin' rollin' down a river
Sealed in red mitochondrial reels
Mama's helix keeps us real
Rockin' steady
Callin' this song exactly what it is.

Hummin' all kinds of
Medicinal lullabies up in here.

Lips, nose eyes, ears, crown
Tether four extensions down
How great thou art
Poets, dancers, musicians
Scientists, farmers, mathematicians.

Paying dues
Crossing toll booths
In route to missed trees
Sometimes crude
But adores the magic of
Molding hues of you
Baby!

READING GUIDE

Is civilization the renunciation of instinct?

In my previous work, *SYNCHRONICITY: The Oracle of Sun Medicine*, the story "Preface of Three Women", Dr. Francis Cress Welsing, a third-generation Black psychiatrist in her family, spoke of her mind's computer alerting her to an answer via a book title through the library window. In the same story Peggy McIntosh asked if my experience locating her article on racism was otherworldly. "Yes, it was", I said. She then admits her questions regarding racism were answered in her dreams.

The Body, may be considered otherworldly, but I have no other way to share this world I've experienced with you. Perhaps it is for those who live on multiple dimensions; there are many of us.

"In the Times of Old" takes hold of physiologic tenets that imply, as an elderly Buddhist priest said,
> *There were infinite numberless tactful ways using parabolic expressions and reasoning to expound The Word.*

For the pantheist, no one is excluded from this world. It is inclusive of many spiritual beings that promulgate our legacy as hue-mans. I consider myself a Pantheist. The world is fascinating.

In the **"Ishtar Arrives Uninvited"** story, Ishtar's name is spelled and spoken upon awakening from a dream. She was a historical deity. It seems spiritual entities return whispering wrongs done with global implications.

- How is your seeing being judged? By whose ontologic identity, philosophy, theology, belief? Review, "The Body Is Not Just a Sack of Blood".

- How do you judge what you've seen or experienced as otherworldly?
- Is your way of seeing considered a "sin"? Sin, literally means, "to miss the mark."
- Write a poem about yourself or someone you know that may be considered "different."
- What would be your definition of a psychic or sick psychic? Would a sick psychic *always need to continuously harm themselves or others?*
- *Read previous book, Synchronicity: The Oracle of Sun Medicine* and western judgement of sick psychic(s) in "Eyes So Bright" or "Take Me Home Mama".
- Do you see entities or auras around people as in, "Beware of Omission"? Journal that story for review. How old were you when it first occurred?
- Has your body intuited something beyond your trained conscious mind you've doubted, yet later you find to be true? Review poem, "Instinct", or "Language & False Assumptions"
- Learn to release guilt regarding your body's mortal envelope. Listen to it.
- Come as a child welcoming your sensory. Review, "Light Medicine", or "Halloween at Seek".
- What distress signals has your body shared but you unwittingly ignore then submit to later as in, "This Little Light of Mine" or "Instinct"?
- If we accept the body is *born broken*, will it ignore gifts our bio-electromagnetic shell offers like the poem, "Gifts Not Forgotten", that speaks of body sensing truths?

Gabor Maté, MD questioned the ideology that believes diseases are purely physical, diseases happen to the organs, diseases are not socially stressed, and politics, science, and medicine are not of their systemic causation.

We can review Orwell's thought with that vein that, "…an effect can become a cause, <u>reinforcing</u> the original cause, producing the same effect in an intensified form…indefinitely."

The poem, "Beware of Omission" speaks of an entity appearing just before invading a relative's body, causing symptoms of lethargy to appear. Cultural "witch doctors" know of cultural toxins that invade the body's aura to disrupt it from functioning well.

Merely contemplating the chaos may be the will of some, but not in causal traditions. There are reasons for everything.

The term, extra sensory perception, e.g. in "Remembering Childhood", "The Aftermath", "Instinct", or "The Lamp", speak of the body's defense or immunity intelligence.

These are but a few poems that aid in recovery of the authentic self that will make you laugh, cry, and/or say WTF is going on with the sensory systems of this world

I hope you find these stories an act of resistance from deadening our senses so we can reinstate our interior.

The Body oracle of Memory is after all an insurance policy against loss.

ACKNOWLEDGMENTS

First, to Great Mystery of all living beings for the act of magic within *The Body: Oracle of Memory* that selects congruent times in rhymes that measures issues in body's tissues speak. To parents who allowed me to listen and pay attention to all life that surrounds us, and for my daughter, her father, and our agreement to learn systems and techniques of communication via religion and education, through joy and pain's enlightenment

To Ancestors for your talents, genius, warmth, and commitment to activism that will continue to live with us for generations to come. Honored to have known you, and have you share the lessons of your craft.
Amiri Baraka
Octavia Butler
Toni Morrison
QR Hand
Jack Hirschman
Al Young

John Sims, you left us too soon but left a legacy of genius activism with quilt titled "Pi" that will honor the cover of the Patrice Lumumba Anthology published by Nomadic Press and EastSide Arts Alliance for generations to come.

To Octavia Butler and Toni Morrison, my reflective TM, who eloquently demonstrated the mark of blood water's mystery, reincarnating, transmutating, and transmitting uninvited spirits that come demanding to be heard like, "Ishtar Arrives Uninvited", "Miriam Makeba", "Body Aftermath", and "This Little Light." Your work has given me permission move outside the status-quo, for this I am abundantly grateful and thankful to have known you and your work.

Immense gratitude for editors, Michaela Mullin, Diane Goettel, and Angela Leroux-Lindsey for your six eyes seeing what I could not. To Lorraine Bonner, artist of image titled, Clearing the Channels that set this tome off to its other-worldly place. So honored you agreed to collaborate your gift with me; and to Diane Goettel for contracting Lorraine Bonner's work I selected for *The Body: Oracle of Memory*.

Many thanks to J.K. Fowler, Nomadic Press, and Michaela Mullin, for the years of service to the BIPOC writing community. We regret Nomadic Press had to close yet thankful J.K. provided a new home for our work. We extend heartfelt gratitude to Diane Goettel of Black Lawrence Press in New York for continuing to accept our work for publication.

Grateful for the following collaborations with whom some of the contents of *The Body: Oracle of Memory* has been shared. Joyce Gordan Gallery in Oakland, Museum of the African Diaspora in SF, EastSide Arts Alliance-Patrice Lumumba aka Holla Back in Oakland, Medicine for Nightmares in SF, Manifest Differently in SF, Lit Quake, Beast Crawl, and Lit Crawl of SF Bay Area, San Francisco Public Library, SF de Young Museum, City Lights Publishers, SF, Revolutionary Poets Brigade, The Beat Museum-SF, Bird and Beckett in SF, SF State U., Nomadic Press Open Mic, Sacred Grounds, Get Lit, Oakland Museum, San Jose Poetry Center, Beautiful Black Books, Tarot in Pandemic & Revolution, Luis Jordon at Large, Oakland Maroons, Black Arts Movement in Oakland, Oakland Asian Cultural Center, The Malonga Casquelourd Center for the Arts in Oakland, BAMFA Berkeley Art Museum Film Archive of CA., Breaking Down Walls, Bellmont Poetry in Bellmont, Womanicity Radio International-Hawaii, Stanford U.—Poets by the Bay, San Jose State U.- Diasporic Peoples Writing Collective, Moon Drops Collective, Black and Brown Club, African & African American Museum and Library-Oakland, and all the open mics that Zoomed locally across the country and continents delivering the word.

To Eleanor Longden for her Ted Talk, The Voices in My Head and to all Comrades in arms that continue the good fight to release, search, police, study, heal, and craft the word in our own unique *say*. So appreciate you! You're too numerous to name but you know who you are! Truly Thankful we agreed to share this red road together!

Grateful to the following publishers and E-zines of my work.

"James Baldwin Spoke Loud that Day", published in *Second Stutter Volume Five*, anthology San Francisco 2020. A series of Baldwin's word work echoes a quote sent one day via email before heading to the market regarding the entitled refusal to see abuse within layers of society.

"Tale Tells of Genocide" published by Vagabond in *Revolutionary Vision* 2022, anthology. Prose work reflects series of intuitive collective consciousness connections beginning with the book *We Charge Genocide* and all the groups that came forth within days of one another repeating the same words.

"Is The Body Just a Sack of Blood" versions published in *Uncommon Ground* by Pease Press and *Colossus: Freedom* by Colossus Press. Much Gratitude to that voice that resonated so profoundly that it stopped a 14-year-old from taking her life and gave the ability to share the story that encourages others with those same thoughts to stop and recognize there are many far worse off than us. Suicide is up 600%.

"Little Light Shines," published in, *The Town* anthology, by Nomadic Press 2023. To the body that empathized with other bodies sacrificing gold fluid at plasma center while a single mother discerns her role for survival.

"Breaking Bread Burden," published by Kallatumba Press 2022 *Storm Warning,* anthology. Poem reviews WWII Black veteran returning home from the war and his recollection of being treated worse than those called the enemy.

"Umum Bumum & Sumum", published by *Second Stutter -Volume Five*, SF 2020 anthology. The title of the poem comes from English language learners reasoning the buy-bull. The poem agrees in its speech.

"Suffer Little Children," from Workers in Cane, Spy Boy- art by Lavar Monroe, published by Museum of African Diaspora, 2019 exhibit Coffee Sugar Rum. Ekphrastic poem tells of children forced to work in the cane fields in threat of losing life or limbs.

"Scent Sentenced," published by *Digital Papers*, 2022. UCB Bay Area Writing Project. Observes a child remembering his beginnings, from amphibian to human.

"Toddler's Iron Memory," published by *Digital Papers*, 2022. UCB Bay Area Writing Project. Observes a child noticing one of eight antique irons at an old clothes cleaner.

"In The Be," published by *Digital Papers*, and The Maynard 2020 speaks to the art of being.

"The Ritual," published by *Digital Papers*, 2021. UCB Bay Area Writing Project. Poem weaves consistency of being into increasingly ignored ritual of existence.

Tureeda Ture Ade Mikell, Story Medicine Woman, author, activist for holism, called 'word magician,' is an award-winning poet, published nationally and internationally. Qigong Healer, workshop leader, storyteller, lyricist, performance artist, founder of The Tree of Life Foundation H.L.P. , advocate for youth and adults. Published over 70 student anthologies with CA Poets in the Schools since 1989. Performed in schools, libraries and universities, Google, Genentech, Aspire, Lawrence Hall, and Golden Gate Academy of Sciences, Randall, Oakland, and De Young Museums. Was featured spoken word artist at SOAN [Soul of a Nation] Exhibit, and the American Academy of Poets, Fire Thieves, at the De Young, and Museum of the African Diaspora, (MoAD) Lit-Quake Afrofuturism. Featured storyteller for the 55 Year Anniversary of the Black Panther Party, National Association of Black Storytellers, featured poet storyteller celebrating Octavia Butler's 70th birthday, and Eth-Noh-Tec Nu Wa Delegate storyteller in Beijing, China in collaboration with the University of Beijing. Recent publications of her work can be found in, *Black Fire This Time* (Willow Press, 2022), *Revolutionary Poets Brigade*, *Second Stutter* (City Lights, 2022) *Common Ground* (Pease Press, 2022) and many more.

Her full length collection, *Synchronicity, The Oracle of Sun Medicine*, was released in 2020, and nominated for the California Book Award. She is also co-curator of the *Patrice Lumumba Anthology*, released in 2021 by Nomadic Press, both now at Black Lawrence Press.

Has been said, "Tureeda is hell bent on asserting life."